Echoes of Wisdom.....
What We Know Now

In Collaboration with
Susie De Giusti and Heather Andrews

Foreword By Jessica Soodeen
A Special Testimony by Wendy Bélanger

Featuring:

Carmen Davidson
Danielle Shantz
Erica Bearss
Jackie McCoy
Jennifer Gordon
Jessica Lee
Jessica Soodeen
Linh Tran
Lisa Sobry
Melissa Mazurek
Shona Welsh

Echoes of Wisdom
Copyright © 2024 Susie De Giusti
TGIF- Towards Gainful Infinite Freedom

All rights reserved. Printed in the United States of America and Canada. No part of this book may be used or reproduced in any manner whatsoever without written permission from the author, except in the case of brief quotations within critical articles or reviews.

The compilers and publisher have made extensive efforts to ensure that the information was correct at time of release. The compilers, authors and publisher do not assume and disclaim any liability to any party as the written content of this book is based on co-authors expertise and experiences. We assume no responsibility for errors or omissions in the information in this book.

You should only use this information as you see fit at your own risk. Your life and circumstances may not be suited to these examples with what we share within these pages. The author and publisher are neither doctors nor in the position of registered authorities to give you expert advice.

The names and details have been changed to maintain privacy of some parties mentioned. How you choose to use the information in this book within your own life is completely your own responsibility and own risk.

Print ISBN: 978-1-7387166-1-6
Ebook ISBN: 978-1-7387166-3-0

Publishing Coach Heather Andrews
Editing Jennifer Traynor/Proofreading Manita Ramos
Book Cover Lorie Miller Hanson

Acknowledgments

This compilation could not have happened without the hard work of each person who has had a hand in the making of *Echoes of Wisdom*. It would not exist without all the beautiful souls that contributed a chapter. Thank you to Carmen Davidson, Danielle Steiert Shantz, Erica Bearss, Heather Andrews, Jackie McCoy, Jennifer Gordon, Jessica Lee, Jessica Soodeen, Linh Tran, Lisa Sobry, Melissa Mazurek, Shona Welsh, and Wendy Bélanger.

Heather Andrews, thank you for taking me under your wing and believing in my idea of *Echoes of Wisdom*. Without you, I could not have brought forth these beautiful, engaging, and inspiring stories, nor could I have started my journey as an author. Words are piling up as I continue my writing journey.

To Jennifer Traynor, thank you for your expertise in grammar, editing, and all-around proofing extraordinaire. Your patience and guidance with each of us is and has been priceless.

Thank you to the talented and brilliant Lorie Miller Hanson. Your design truly resonates and captures the title of this compilation along with the ideas and suggestions of each author.

Echoes of wisdom are always being passed down from ancestors. We unconsciously choose to take it or not. Sometimes we are required to understand the wisdom through our own experiences. There are no "bad" decisions in life; there are only wrong decisions that move us along our journey. Paulo Coelho said it brilliantly in his book entitled *Eleven Minutes*:

"Everything tells me that I am about to make a wrong decision, but making mistakes is just part of life. What does the world want of me? Does it want me to take no risks, to go back where I came from because I didn't have the courage to say 'yes' to life?"

Each of the authors in this book said yes to their life and their way of learning each step of the way.

So, dear reader, I not only thank you for partaking in my and each author's journey, but I also ask you to give yourself the grace to be open to learning from us. Choose wisely as you say "yes" to life by making it the best you possibly can. If you fall, know that we are here to pick you up and cheer you on along your journey.

With love and much gratitude,
Susie De Giusti

Table of Contents

Foreword
By Jessica Soodeen 1

Introduction 5

A Special Testimony to Perseverance
By Wendy Bélanger 7

Chapter 1
Victim Mode to Victory Mode
By Carmen Davidson 16

Chapter 2
Embracing the Evolution of Family
By Danielle Shantz 27

Chapter 3
Bootcamp For Your Brain!
By Erica Bearss 36

Chapter 4
Let Love Lead You
By Heather Andrews 48

Chapter 5
Perfection Isn't the Damn Goal
By Jackie McCoy 58

Chapter 6
A Survivor's Journey Through Self-Love and Healing
By Jennifer Gordon 67

Chapter 7
The Art of Forgiveness at Full Throttle
By Jessica Soodeen 78

Chapter 8
Dare to Dream
By Jessica Lee 87

Chapter 9
If Only We Had More Money
By Linh Tran 96

Chapter 10
Finding My Personal Power
By Lisa M. Sobry 105

Chapter 11
If Only I Had Known: The Journey Back Home to Myself
By Melissa Dawn Mazurek 116

Chapter 12
Claiming My Confidence
By Shona Welsh 126

Chapter 13
Finding Grace Amid Life's Shittiest Moments
By Susie De Giusti 137

Conclusion 146

Foreword

By Jessica Soodeen

There is a fine line between reflection and regret. The energy around both is quite different, yet we can ruminate on either of them in a journey to find meaning. The analytical side of our brains slices and dices situations into smaller pieces, and our hearts bounce around in the various emotions which bubble to the surface in this process. This IS life! Regret does not serve, and luckily when we go there, it is possible to acknowledge and pivot. This is the cornerstone of reframing and is paramount in learning to *feel* through the tough times, to recognize the lessons if there are any, and to move on with a deeper sense of understanding.

This type of reframing is where real transformation has space to occur. What does this transformation look like for you? It could show up in your relationship with yourself, it may drive next-level growth in your business, or maybe you've come to a perspective of heightened compassion. Rising through levels of compassion is the difference between saying, "I feel how you feel" and "I appreciate how you feel." It is avoiding potential emotional empathy fatigue and shifting to truly holding space. Realizing that perfection isn't the goal, but instead, it's being able to draw lessons and subsequently support others in their journeys that bring the fulfillment of purpose.

Echoes of Wisdom is a tapestry of insights that exists in the realm of reflection. The subtitle of the book, "What We Know Now" should be viewed through a lens of growth and insight!

Within each chapter, the authors take you on a journey of resilience and courage, rather than down the roads of remorse and guilt. One of the most compelling aspects of these stories is the authors' ability to delve into deeply relatable life happenings. In this compilation, you will read about facing cancer during a pandemic, immigration narratives, chronicles of working in a man's world, tales of re-invention after fallout, and much more! Be ready to laugh, cry, be inspired, gain insight, and be amazed. The chapters that follow include lessons and tools to overcome obstacles that life throws at us.

It's a privilege to write alongside these incredible authors! Each woman demonstrates grit and how to find joy in their life odyssey, regardless of whether their emotions were those of happiness, sadness, anger, frustration, peace, or the like. These women also show how perfection isn't the goal in this life, nor is being "happy" all the time. The concept of being in a state of JOY in good times and bad has been a game changer for me in so many facets of my life. The women who wrote in this book exemplify a true sense of vulnerability and share their experiences of a plethora of emotions that are presented in their stories. Struggle, grief, sadness… these are places to visit, not in which to stay. And, if you can get to a place of joy, then those visits come with a sense of perspective that facilitates reinvention and renewal.

My own motorsports background started with motorcycles in my hometown of Calgary; however, it took me overseas to work with cars. This was a huge shift out of my comfort zone. Not only was I working with vehicles with 4 wheels instead of 2, but I was also far away from family and needed to learn a new language or two! It was through JOY that I was able to face the loneliness and the longing for familiarity. Touching base with my mom proved to be the grounding I needed!

In closing, Heather Andrews and Susie De Giusti have gathered an incredible group of women to participate in this heartfelt project to share wisdom. I'm humbled to have been able to welcome you, the reader, to this exciting tapestry of adventures. Buckle up and enjoy the ride!

Jessica Soodeen, Speaker and Compassion Architect

Believe by Richard Paul

I just want to start again and believe..
Believe in a life that has no reasons to grieve.

Believe in honesty and trust and everything that is good…
No evil, misfortunes or superstitions: never a reason to knock on wood.

Believe in fantasy and all things that are magical and true…..
No atrocities or fear; everything is enchanting and mystical, never blue.

Believe in destiny, innocence, religion, faith and hope..
No doubts, misgivings or suspicions; just the ability to pray and cope.

Believe in paradise, joy, laughter, happiness, peace of mind…..
No mediocrity or incompetence; nothing is unspeakable and everyone is kind.

Believe in true love, there will be no heartache and pain…
No sorrow, sadness, worries or woe; there is nothing to feign.

Believe in the unbelievable, a place that will always be safe and secure…
No abuse, foul play or wrongs; all things are equal, marvelous, wonderful and pure.

Believe in tomorrows, new beginnings; discover the wonderment of each new day..
No judgments, labels or guilt; there are always choices and you do have a say.

Believe all things are possible and true, no limitations as to what can be…
No despair or hopelessness; unlimited potential in all that you see.

I just want to start again and believe….
I just want to find a way to believe in me.

Author of Love, Life and In Between

Introduction

Life is a journey of unexpected twists, trials, triumphs, and moments of deep reflection. In *Echoes of Wisdom*, 14 brave and insightful women come together to share their most personal stories of growth, self-discovery, and resilience. Through their diverse experiences—from overcoming failed marriages to navigating immigration, from the highs of financial success to the lessons learned in struggles—they offer a collective voice of wisdom that speaks to the heart of every woman.

This collaboration serves as a beacon of hope for women of all ages, particularly younger women who may be embarking on their own journeys of self-discovery. Too often, society paints a picture of perfection that fails to reflect the complexities of real life. But the authors of *Echoes of Wisdom* offer a candid portrayal of the truth—strength is born through adversity and wisdom is gained through the challenges we sometimes fear the most.

These stories are not simply reflections of personal hardships or victories. They are shared with the purpose of inspiring, uplifting, and reminding every reader that they are not alone in their struggles or uncertainties. Each author brings her own perspective, yet a common thread runs through their narratives: the importance of self-love. Whether through the dissolution of relationships, the uprooting of life through immigration, or the emotional toll of financial hardships, these women have learned to find strength within themselves. In learning to love themselves, they discovered the key to true fulfillment and the resilience to move forward.

The stories in this book will resonate with women from all walks of life. Perhaps you've faced the devastation of coming from a broken home. Or maybe you've fought the battle with cancer and won. Or, like some, you've had to start fresh by moving to a new city or creating a business from scratch, all the while wondering if success will ever come. Whatever the experience, the women in *Echoes of Wisdom* have been there, and their stories are living proof that healing, growth, and triumph are possible.

More than a collection of stories, *Echoes of Wisdom* is a testament to the resilience of the human spirit. These pages are filled with raw honesty and heartfelt truths, but they are also imbued with hope. It is a book that calls upon women to stand tall in the face of adversity, embrace their own journeys with courage, and draw strength from the wisdom that each experience brings.

As you read these pages, we invite you to reflect on your own life with its challenges and victories. May these stories encourage you to embrace your own wisdom, and to know that no matter where you are on your journey, you are never alone.

Come on the journey with us!
Susie and Heather

A Special Testimony to Perseverance
There is Always a Choice!

By Wendy Bélanger, Celebrity Stylist

Over the years, I have delivered speeches at leadership conferences, hair shows, and other audiences about how I grew my business to what it is today. The journey may have looked easy; however, there is always the background that no one ever sees.

I was asked to write an expert opinion and share my echoes of wisdom; this is what I know.

I am a hairdresser who travels the world doing hair. I have done hair for the Oscars, Emmys, MTV Music Awards, Fashion Week, and well-known celebrities. I own two salons, and the real estate they are located in. I am a mom to a beautiful boy who is 26 years old and is a successful music producer. I am more than lips and lashes. Yes, that is cheeky. I smile as I write this.

This story is about a journey of getting from A to B. We know what "B" looks like so let's talk about "A". I have many of what I call "excuses", not reasons, to not be where I am right now. Often, I hear people say, "The reason I did not achieve this or that is because this happened or that." I have had many life experiences that I could have let define my future, but I did not. I could have stayed where I was and let the reasons be my barricade.

To name a few, my sister died when I was 20; she was my best friend. I was in a car accident that could have taken my career away. The message here is every time something happened, I decided not to let the experience define me. I made a choice. I would not have the success I do if I had let life occurrences be my reasons and define me. They would have been my excuses. The bottom line is you can really overcome anything. All you have to do is choose.

As a celebrity hair stylist, and owner of the award-winning hair salon, Influence, the road may have looked easy from an outside perspective. But that couldn't be further from the truth, though I can tell you it has been worth it. Along the path, there were things I might have changed and others that could not be changed as it was the journey of learning that I needed for me to achieve the success I have now.

All day long, I listen to stories of trials and tribulations from guests sitting in my salon chair. Some have traumatic experiences, and it hurts my heart to know that they are debilitated by this. Sometimes I wish the hair appointments were hours longer so I could help them. I have learned that when you put one foot forward, there will be an answer or opportunity that moves you along your path. You just have to trust there is more for you.

Growing up in Saskatchewan, my dad had a very successful career. He wanted the same for me; to attend university after high school. In my heart, I knew this was not what I wanted, and was unsure of my career path. Since I was always doing my friends' hair, my dad suggested I go to hair school. To me, it sounded like a good plan.

Within the month, I was accepted and off I went as a young woman to Saskatoon to begin my new career. Needless to say, it was my first time away from home and I spent more time going out at night with girlfriends and I missed more school than I care to admit. It was a nine-month program. I was allowed to miss one day per month, and if I missed more than that, I would owe $25.00 per day. I had two months of school left and I owed $1,000.00. I was suspended from school for a week. My father told me that I would have to support myself and get a job. I did not learn anything from this suspension as I spent my week going out to the club.

I did not listen to the universe's lesson, so it decided to hit me harder. On the last day of my suspension, I was driving to my first day of work. I came around the corner, and up ahead I noticed a car come into my lane. We were about to have a head-on collision! I waited till the final second; I swerved left into oncoming traffic. I remember feeling the swoosh in my hair as I missed the oncoming car, and the Jeep began to spin. Then the back of the Jeep hit the curb, went up, hit a tree, and then the back seat, because it wasn't bolted in properly, came out and hit us from behind. Essentially, we were rear-ended three times in the same accident. I remember my sister coming to visit me in the hospital. We were so close. She sat on the edge of my bed and said to me, "Don't you die on me; we have so much life left to live."

The emergency room doctor told me I was very lucky to be alive. I was encouraged to take time off work to heal. I asked about going back to school, he said that was fine. He then asked what I was taking. I said, "I am going to be a hairdresser." He said, "Oh baby girl, you may have to reconsider that. You were rear-ended three times in this accident and you injured the exact muscles you will need for your career." That's when I realized I wanted to be a hairdresser. Quitting was not going to be my destiny. After being off for two months, I joined a gym to rehabilitate my back. I went back to school and became a prize student in the program.

I knew this was my second chance. I got my first job in a salon, and I figured I was on my way.

As the year passed, my sister got pregnant, and I was so excited to be an auntie.

Who knew what would happen next?

My sister went into labor and her baby was on the way. I went to meet her at the hospital for what was supposed to be an amazing experience for us. It did not turn out that way. There were complications during her caesarean and she died after my niece was born. It was one year from the day of my accident where she sat on my hospital bed.

I can't even tell you the grief I felt. This was my sister. Her life was taken too soon. We had memories and experiences to make, and she was my best friend.

I sat in the dark for many days thinking about how I didn't want to be here or wondering how I would do life on my own.

To go through this pain, seemed unbearable. As the days passed, I realized my sister would not want me to give up. She would want me to live my life. My family had lost one person, and my sister would be disappointed if I hurt myself. I knew I had to find the strength to carry on.

Quitting would not be my story. Excuses are not reasons to quit.

Day by day, I moved forward. I got married and had a baby of my own. When my son was two years old, I worked part-time at a hair salon; it was three weeks till our possession of our new home. Life seemed to be on track until one Friday night my husband made a choice which showed me, he no longer wanted to be married to me. Devastation filled my heart. Once again, I had to make a choice; roll over in my grief or move forward. I waited a week, came down the stairs, and said, "It's over. I will move into the house, and I will take all of our debt with me so if we settled this in court, it would be fair. I don't want any child support. I don't want any alimony; all I ever want and will ever ask of you is that you be a good dad because we ruined us but we created our son and we are responsible for him having a good life regardless of our situation." We decided to divorce and mutually reached an agreement, we created a win-win situation to provide our child with a good life. We've only had three disagreements in the 24 years of being divorced. Our child would not be a statistic. My son has grown to be a good man with a great career in the music industry. I am so proud. He is a wise kid. He once said," When breaking up, parents should never involve the kids. Don't bad mouth the other parent as the kids are half of each of you. If you bad mouth the parent, you are badmouthing your child." I realized in that moment that I would never be able to change the fact that Jonah would one day tell the story about me. But I knew what I could do was change the story that he told. I went back to work full-time and started my life over.

I didn't want to let what happened change the fact that I had the following goals:

1. I wanted to work for a manufacturer.
2. I wanted to teach salon professionals.
3. I wanted to have my own salon, all before I was 30.

One month before my 30th birthday, I opened Influence Salon.

I remember feeling helpless many times growing my business. My friend once asked me, "What are you worried about?" I told her I was afraid, and asked "What if I can't do this?" She said, "Go there, play it out in your mind; what you are afraid of? Fear is of the unknown. Figure out what you would do and then you won't be afraid anymore."

So, I played it out, found a solution, and the anxiety went away. I use this practice to this day.

Influence Salon has a deeply respected mentorship program to help hairdressers thrive. It means I can pay it forward.

We believe in client service which makes us unique for so many reasons.

Once Influence was running itself with a great team in place, I'd become artistic director of a multi-million-dollar company. I had a visa to travel to the U.S. to do celebrities' hair at events like the Oscars, Emmys, and MTV Music Awards. I had my dream job.

Yet, I was away the majority of the time. My salon was operated by managers. Before COVID-19, I was doing famous people's hair, attending conferences, and was on 90 flights a year. Some would say I was living the dream.

When the pandemic happened, I could no longer travel and felt like I was no longer a famous hairdresser. I realized I had made that my identity and did not know who I was at home. I had to start over again. This is one of my biggest life lessons. Who am I? It took some time, but I realized is what truly matters to me is my company, being at home, and creating a personal life for myself. It's not often that you get to rewrite who you are, but the opportunity presented itself and I took it.

Quitting was not going to be my story.

I have taken the time to reflect on the lessons I've learned and applied them to the choices I've made. This is what I've accomplished, and continue to work and focus on:

- I have become a priority in my life. I choose Wendy.
- I am building my business, and I get to help people create the life they want. I share the lessons that I've learned with them.
- I bought another space and put in a salon concept that was a dream of mine for many years.
- I am building the Influence Salon and Identity Express Bar.
- I mentor our team of young professionals to do, have, and be anything they want.
- Our brand's motto is, "Experience the difference."
- Passion creates purpose.
- It's important to make mental health and self-care a priority while creating healthy experiences, so you can finish strong and proudly stand tall.

Whatever your story is, you are not alone. There is a way through the challenges you might face. Solutions can be found. You may not see it right away, but it is there. I have learned that the more you pay attention to negative things, the more negativity will come your way. Adopt a positive mindset. If you can find your inner motivation, and mix it with vulnerability and active choices, then you can make it through.

You are your choices, not your excuses. You get to rewrite your story. You get to Do, Have and, Be anything you want in your life.

Wendy Bélanger
Celebrity Hair Stylist and CEO of Influence the Salon and Identity the Express Bar

Connect with Wendy:

https://linktr.ee/wendybelanger?utm_source=qr_code

Walking the Talk

Carmen Davidson

Carmen Davidson is a devoted mother, multidisciplinary artist, and author from Ontario, Canada who shares her journey of healing and self-discovery. With a deep-rooted commitment to conscious living, she shares her transformative experiences through her writing. Driven by a curious passion for ayurvedic healing and ancient esoteric wisdom, Carmen has courageously transformed personal adversity, including the harrowing impacts of emotional abuse, trauma and toxic codependency, into beacons of hope and inspiration.

Her story is a testament to the human spirit's resilience, inviting readers to explore the depths of their own souls and embark on a path toward inner freedom. Through self-awareness, creative expression, and a profound understanding of subconscious patterns, Carmen empowers women to break free from the chains of past trauma and cultivate authentic, fulfilling relationships grounded in truth.

Connect with Carmen:

https://linktr.ee/carmengd

Chapter 1

Victim Mode to Victory Mode

By Carmen Davidson

I remember the night I was forced against the hood of the police cruiser and reluctantly handcuffed by an officer on this frenzied domestic call. Feeling the cold metal of the restraints pulling on my wrists behind me, I was placed in the back seat of the cruiser. I glanced out the window at my children who were in tears while standing by their father.

How could life pivot from a pleasant family dinner to the unimaginable? Not having food on the table at six o'clock sharp caused an eruption of reactions. Feeling worn down by constant emotional abuse and at the end of my rope, I finally snapped! I aggressively threw a plate of spaghetti at my ex-husband, igniting a forceful struggle for the phone—911 was called, and within a matter of minutes, I was ripped from my family. Arrested and placed in a cold dark cell behind bars was an experience I'd never thought I would have. The feeling of exhaustion and nauseousness came over me like a heavy wave. I felt defeated, like a little girl trying to come up for air but was too far from the surface.

My naive innocence didn't see it coming; my life turned into a turbulent storm and all I could think was, "How the hell did I get HERE?"

I learned soon after that I wasn't the only one this had happened to. Many times, silent abuse goes unnoticed. According to the

What We Know Now

Government of Canada, in 2022, 44% of women reported experiencing domestic abuse.

After such a traumatic experience, I began to take a good look at myself. Why did I tolerate the years of abuse? How did I manage to live with someone's narcissistic behavior for so long? Where did my boundaries go? How did I lose my sense of self, physically, mentally, and emotionally? Functioning from codependency and in a highly dysregulated place for so long became normalized. Post-traumatic stress disorder (PTSD) started to reveal itself.

At 19, I felt I was the most precious princess as he charmingly sought me out, wined and dined me, and swept me off my feet. My belief system at that point was to seek security. I had searched for someone to love and marry me because I wanted to start a family. You know… the old paradigms and societal norms of what's expected. After graduating from college, he put an apartment together for us. I had no say in the matter because he had looked after everything. I thought I found it all! We married shortly after, to begin our fairy-tale life full of promises. This relationship defined me. Not knowing what the boundaries were, I had no idea who I was letting myself become.

Growing up, my father was in and out of the picture. We moved a lot and the constant upheaval as a child, with no stable father figure to learn from, created significant insecurity. This fueled the symptoms of PTSD, and I became withdrawn. I started to live with a blurred lens of what was real and true at the time, clinging to what made me feel safe and secure.

I was an artistic child whose gifts were never fully embraced. I didn't know who I was, what to believe or where I belonged. Self-love was not taught, and emotional health was not nurtured. The real tragedy was that I lived in fear of being alone. That empty feeling of not being enough was a gap of insecurity, waiting to be filled. My subconscious beliefs were adopted from a very young age where I was programmed to survive and bypass my emotions. All I wanted was to meet my foundational needs for safety and security which I so longed for.

After deciding to have children, my relationship of codependency expanded to a deeper level, and the wounds grew more painful. I was a working mom doing the best I could with what I knew at the time. Motherhood was something I loved so much, but without self-worth, I put myself last on the scale of importance. The need to protect my children became increasingly apparent. They were young, vulnerable, and seeking a stable role model. I knew at my core that I had to shift to create structure and security for them. As time went on, the wheel of control cycled, and I was feeling suffocated and powerless.

A narcissist knows how to convince you that you are perfect for each other. Some days felt light, fluid, and easy; while others felt heavy, dark, and confusing. I now know this is due to common narcissistic tendencies, which include manipulation, control, and a lack of empathy. I knew he was suffering internally, but I just didn't know at what level. Ultimately, these behavior patterns show up from complex layers of unresolved past trauma. Narcissists are unaware and uninterested in seeing the impact of their words and actions.

Living with narcissism equaled a life full of conditions and isolation. I became climatized to walking on eggshells to avoid creating friction, as the signs of militant control created such distress in my body. My nervous system became more dysregulated, and the feelings of unworthiness, fear, and doubt continued to grow. I just wanted to be heard. Letting myself be an open target for emotional attacks and believing I could never manage on my own kept me off balance. It is said that when someone frequently recounts how incapable they are, it creates a gradual erosion of self-worth, and they buy into this belief that it is true. Feeling trapped, I became withdrawn. My hopes of a deserving prosperous life for myself withered. My narrative became, "I'll just exist."

My fun, easygoing personality changed, and I became a person I disliked. Despite the turbulence, which I unknowingly allowed, I still believed I was in love. My dedication to remaining faithful, loyal, and giving it my all, was happening no matter what. My parents divorced when I was young, and the instability really affected me. Not wanting to break the family unit, staying together seemed like what was best for my children. Illusively, I hung onto my dreams that everything would turn out okay. But soon enough, I found the daily pressure I put on myself was taking a toll.

I was a born artist who had stopped creating. An expressive part of me was waiting to burst. Tapping into my creativity again was the answer to my heaviness at the time. The therapeutic energy of painting and drawing helped me channel my emotions and enlighten my reality. Yet, the more time I invested in my work, creative hobbies, friendships, and family, the tighter his grip seemed to get. Confidence and independence are threats to someone with a narcissistic nature. He was jealous, insecure, and intimidated. Whenever I would make incredible masterpieces, he would take any chance he could to crumble my value and worth.

At the time, I struggled to mirror a confident role model. Even with creating art, it was difficult to fully process my emotions in a healthy way. I was never taught how to do that. I knew this was something I needed to grasp. I had the desire to grow, so I began a deeper search to reconnect to who I truly was.

The night I was arrested was a turning point for realignment in my life. I knew my marriage was over. A fresh start was on the horizon, and I could taste freedom. Thankfully, the court dropped the assault charges the following day. However, navigating the family legal system was a whole other ballgame. An unbelievable blessing came when I found a shelter offering so much legal aid, assistance, and protection. I accepted the counseling and legal guidance available to me and strengthened my grip on life again. I was able to utilize all the tangible resources, numerous consultations, and therapy to maintain parental stability.

Living at the shelter really began to open my eyes. I wasn't alone, and the sense of support became a healing environment. Over time, I began to envision what life could look like again. My inner worth was reestablished, my strength was reactivated, and the clarity came when I finally felt safe and secure. In 2020/2021, an average of 47,000 people were forced into an emergency shelter to escape domestic violence, according to the Government of Canada. Who knew these types of traumatic experiences would be so common?

Eventually, the court decided to temporarily split child custody between us and our life was slowly reestablished. Breaking free of the legalities felt like a breath of fresh air. I found a new home to rent, made new friends, created new routines, and welcomed a different lens to view life.

Once I understood the reasons why these past experiences came into my life, I realized it was time to find ways to start the process of inner healing. The initial steps were to face the childhood abandonment and emotional damage that was so etched into my being and unpack it on an innermost level. I began to comprehend the level of embodied vulnerability I had and saw the kind of toxic tolerance I was willing to accept.

PTSD is a mental illness commonly talked about when one experiences major trauma in one's life. Identifying how flashbacks, feeling easily startled and emotionally on edge were severe enough, and required treatment to alleviate symptoms.

An evolving step to freedom was finally allowing and receiving help. Coming to terms with the fact that I no longer had to face this journey alone, and the lessons I learned were really blessings in disguise. The support and encouragement from my friends and family showed up in unsurmountable ways. Though it wasn't expressed at the time, gratefulness for all that was available to me was profound. There was no choice but to start believing in myself and my capability to start a new life. Part of trauma recovery includes seeing a favorable future and taking the steps to secure it.

The first big step to beginning my recovery process was participating in a twelve-week "Mindfulness Stress Reduction" course. This intense program teaches you how to reframe your mind and thinking processes. You learn that mindfulness is about living non-judgmentally in the present moment. I began prioritizing my nervous system's health, to maintain a state of rest and digest. The introduction to a daily practice of meditation, breathwork, body scanning, and yoga has been a game changer for me. These healing modalities support the growth of my conscious awareness and regulate the nervous system to function in a state of coherence. Expanding my Ayurvedic and somatic practices with deeper meditation, therapeutic touch, aromatherapy, sound therapy, tapping, and earthing all have become part of my ongoing healing which helps on a deeper cellular level. Somatic practices connect the heart, mind, and body to help you listen and feel any internal discomfort or imbalances to release emotions. Common practices include tai chi, qigong, therapeutic touch, and massage—all of which I have used to help navigate greater healing.

Simply leading a healthier lifestyle has been my core focus for overall healing and wellness. Consuming organic whole foods, drinking alkaline water, practicing daily movement, and prioritizing sufficient rest are some of the many ways I support my daily vitality.

The more conscious I became in my life, the deeper my desire became to create new core values and define my priorities. I created a VISION to help realign myself with what matters most. This vision included clear goals in all four quadrants of my existence—health, relationships, vocation, as well as time and money freedom. My goal was to make decisions on what I would love to bring into my life in alignment with my core values. Clearly identifying what my best life would look like, full of meaning and purpose, was according to my standards and not anyone else's. I defined who I wanted to be in my life in ways I could give back. I looked at where I wanted to be and what I wanted to do that was worthy of joy, peace, and freedom. I set intentions daily, recited positive affirmations with regular meditation, and invested in myself to acquire more wisdom and knowledge. Taking massive action steps in the direction of my vision helped to create my desired results.

Above all, faith and belief have been my anchor. My relationship with spirituality has played a profound part in my healing journey. Learning and practicing meaningful ways to connect with an infinite source bigger than myself has helped me strengthen my path of divinity. It has created a deep sense of belonging, purpose, and interconnectedness and has allowed me to process my life with greater spiritual wisdom and awareness.

I have found the importance of shadow work incredibly valuable. Choosing to unpack the negative ego, the root of my triggers, and the dark side of my decisions, has helped me better understand myself. In doing shadow work, I have been able to experience deep levels of forgiveness towards my ex. Through choosing to heal, I have found greater compassion and kindness in my heart, along with gratitude for the lessons learned.

Some days, healing from years of trauma and codependency can seem endless. The healing journey itself is an evolution and I deeply believe that I could heal from the core by visualizing a positive future. I achieved continued strength through reading, journaling, and doing deep inner work. It was important to rewrite my belief system from the previous stuck paradigms and common hour thinking. My subconscious beliefs became conscious once I realized that I lived and breathed my trauma. I continue to process my emotions and have chosen to consciously change my reality. By listening to my body and paying close attention to when a situation triggers a negative response, I notice when my emotions heighten. By recognizing how it makes me feel, I identify exactly what is causing this emotion to come up. If I keep it in and do not process it, eventually it will burst into a reaction. Responding with a positive mindset helps build the inner strength and resilience to look at fear, doubt, or anger straight in the face. Being patient and holding compassion for myself while I take the time required to unpack the layers of deep emotional wounds are part of my continual healing. Seeking professional guidance and surrounding myself with support have been instrumental in my voyage back to overall clarity and well-being.

Remembering that I am a mirror for my children is pertinent to their growth. For them to heal, I must heal myself. For them to feel worthy and safe, I, myself, must emanate worth and safety. Daily, I continue to be open and curious with a willingness to evolve and grow, with the hope that it encourages them to do the same. I share authentically with them, as we seek spiritual practices together, and share common interests in emotional and physical well-being. Luckily, we were all blessed with the power of graceful resilience and have overcome the many obstacles from the past.

If I knew back then what I know now, I'm sure life would have looked a little different. But then, I wouldn't have the wisdom of experience and the stories to share. My journey has propelled me to make choices that attract true healing. It is possible to rebirth personal power and freedom because I am living the truth of this today. If you have experienced any kind of deep emotional trauma and choose to look at it, breaking free from its grasp can be done. Walking a path of awareness within yourself will lead you to find the keys to unlock new dimensions in your life. Recognize the patterns, set personal boundaries, and believe you are worthy of dynamic health and happiness. You are more powerful and contain more potential than any circumstance, situation, or condition. You have what it takes to experience epic transformation.

This is your life but live it in truth. Only you have the highest authority to make life whatever you want it to be. So, be unstoppable! Don't look back. You only need to look forward to authentically living the life you LOVE.

Danielle Shantz

For as long as Danielle Shantz can remember, she has always wanted to be an educator. Danielle's love for learning and sharing with others is a lifelong passion and crusade to which she devotes her heart and soul. Within her career path as an educator, she has engaged and inspired others as a teacher, learning coach, assessment and data consultant, vice principal, and now as a principal. Her favorite and most important role, however, is being a mom.

Born in Chemainus, British Columbia, and raised in Saskatchewan with her family, her roots are in the Land of the Living Skies. The art of sharing stories comes from her grandfather and father, who instilled in her a love for the art of communication and making connections with everyone you meet. Through these experiences, stories, and the love for learning and educating, the idea of creating a collection of stories, problems, and most importantly solutions, emerged.

As society moves through the birthing canal of a new world and a new life after the pandemic, Danielle believes students, educators, parents, and leaders need a roadmap. This is a cause that has become near and dear to her heart. As we move through the dawn of a new era, much of the impact on our children, educators, education system, and our communities are yet to be determined.

When asked, "Did you always know you wanted to be a teacher?" Danielle's response was, "I used to line the dolls up and then eventually my sisters so that I could teach them. For the life of me, I can not recall just what I was sharing with them, but I am sure it was important."

Connect with Danielle:

https://linktr.ee/DanielleJamieson

Chapter 2

Embracing the Evolution of Family

By Danielle Shantz

Family is a concept that defies a single, universal definition. Personal experiences, cultural contexts, and societal norms shape it. At its core, a family is a group of individuals connected by blood, marriage, adoption, or a sense of mutual commitment and support. Traditionally, a family is thought of as a nuclear unit—two parents and their children. However, this conventional structure is just one of many forms that a family can take.

As society evolves, so does the concept of family. Today, families come in a multitude of configurations: single-parent families, blended families, families with same-sex parents, childless couples, extended families living together, and even close-knit groups of friends can consider themselves a family. Each of these forms reflects the changing dynamics and expanding definitions of what it means to be a family.

The Impact of Change on the Family Unit

A broken family is not necessarily one that is irreparably damaged or dysfunctional. Rather, it is a family that has undergone a significant transformation, leaving it different from what it once was.

In many ways, this brokenness is a natural part of the human experience. Just as individuals grow and change, so do families. The brokenness we feel is often a reflection of our attachment to the way things were, and our struggle to adapt to a new reality. But for those of us who have gone through a significant family unit change, we understand all too well the feelings and processes that we go through while we come out on the other side.

When a family undergoes significant changes—be it through crisis, life-changing events, trauma, or even the natural evolution of relationships—the structure and dynamics of the family unit can shift dramatically. This change can bring about feelings of brokenness, as the familiar patterns and connections are disrupted.

Is the family broken? Yes, in a sense, the family as it once was known is broken. The foundational unit no longer exists in its previous form, and emotions of sadness, anger, and confusion can accompany it. The term "broken" often carries a connotation of irreparability; but in the context of family, it can signify a transformative process rather than an end state.

I recall the many moments leading up to our family unit becoming one of two homes. The dreaded "D" word was about to happen in my life. How can that even be? I never once planned on that being the outcome of my life… of our life. But things are not always what they seem behind closed doors. It was a time of turmoil and grief, yet it was a relief as well. The boys were and continue to remain the center of our decisions, and what is best for them and for all. With their demonstration of resilience and understanding even at a young age, I knew that we would all be okay. Our path would look different and yet we knew in our hearts that we would be better than okay. In fact, their support is what got us through the hardest parts, to be honest. They showed their support by taking turns cooking meals, picking up the slack around the house, and providing an ear to listen when appropriate. We continued to participate in their extracurriculars and travel to tournaments. My family also helped financially.

People will have biased opinions about broken families. When I was a learning coach for our school division, I had an opportunity to rectify the opinion of a young teacher who passed judgment on a student who came from a single-parent family. With smoke coming out of my ears, in an unwavering voice, I said, "How dare you paint children from single-parent homes with the same brush! My children are from a single-parent family. We do not make our family unit an excuse for anything." He later apologized and I told him that I hoped he learned a valuable lesson—that our background and privileged understanding would not work very well in our role as educators. This experience made me realize that there would be others with the same bias. I had gained another tool to help educators, students, and families.

Embracing Change and Moving Forward

The process of navigating through a broken family structure involves acknowledging the pain and uncertainty, as well as recognizing the potential for growth and renewal. This brokenness, while painful, can serve as a catalyst for personal and familial transformation. It allows individuals to reassess their identities, roles, and relationships within the family and to discover new ways of connecting and supporting each other.

For example, in my family, we went through counselling, tons of conversations and tears, of course, but embracing each other where we were in this process was the most important. We took this opportunity to heal and not blame and become anew with each passing day. In fact, my relationship with my sons grew stronger each day. We had each other's back and supported each other through household tasks, sporting events, the continuation of my work as an educator, and the pursuit of our goals as my kids grew and evolved into young men. I recall a few vivid memories as we journeyed on our new path. One evening, we were reading as we always did. My oldest was reading a Max Lucado book and it brought tears to my eyes when he said, "Mom don't worry, God knew before we came here that we would go through this." I was in awe of his understanding at the age of 9 or 10. I was reminded that I had very special young men in my life.

Another memory was when my youngest got his driving license. I was ready to take him to hockey practice like usual when he said to me, "Mom, I got this today." This was a significant event in our life because now he had even more independence. While it was frightening for me, it was exhilarating for him.

When I was doing my master's program, I took a class during the summer which meant it was jam-packed with a lot of learning in a short time. I remember one weekend when I came home with huge binders of information that I needed to go through, but I also wanted to prepare meals for me and my boys. They looked at me, told me not to worry, and made the meals themselves. They looked after everything so I could get all of my assignments done on time. Just another example of a stressful time that my boys helped me get through.

These young men are kind, compassionate, smart, helpful, humorous, and not to mention, handsome. They are well-loved by everyone lucky enough to know them. They make authentic friends wherever they are. I get so many compliments about my boys for all these qualities, but I know it wasn't all me. They have solid, incredible qualities that are truly theirs and have developed along the way.

The Metaphor of the Butterfly

Much like a butterfly emerging from a cocoon, individuals and families can find new forms of existence and harmony after experiencing brokenness. This transformation involves several steps, such as acknowledging the pain and loss, yet also recognizing the potential for growth and renewal. This also includes knowing that healing from the brokenness of a changed family unit is a journey. Here are some steps that can help in this process:

1. **Acknowledgment and Acceptance:** The first step in healing is to acknowledge the pain and accept the reality of the situation. This can be difficult, but it is essential for moving forward. Denial only prolongs the healing process.

2. **Allowing Yourself to Grieve:** Grief is a natural response to loss, and it's important to allow yourself to feel and process your emotions. This might involve crying, talking about your feelings, or finding other ways to express your grief.

3. **Self-Reflection:** Take time to reflect on your feelings and experiences. Journaling can be a helpful tool for this. Write about your thoughts, emotions, and the changes you're going through. This can help you gain clarity and insight into your situation. What you feel is legit and needs to be acknowledged. Let yourself own it and feel it.

4. **Finding Support:** Surrounding yourself with supportive people can make a significant difference. This may include friends, family members, or a therapist. Support groups can also be helpful, as they provide a space to connect with others who are going through similar experiences.

5. **Seeking Help:** Don't hesitate to seek professional help if you need it. A therapist can provide valuable support and guidance as you navigate this challenging time. Therapy can offer a safe space to explore your feelings and develop strategies for coping. It doesn't have to be forever, only in the meantime.

6. **Reimagining Your Identity:** When a family changes, it can challenge your sense of identity. It's important to take time to explore who you are outside of the old family structure. This might involve pursuing new interests, setting new goals, or simply taking time for self-reflection.

7. **Embracing Change:** Change can be difficult, but it can also be an opportunity for growth. Embrace the changes in your family and look for the positive aspects. This might involve creating new traditions, forming new connections, or finding new ways to support each other.

8. **Setting Boundaries:** In the process of redefining your family, it's important to set healthy boundaries. This might involve establishing limits with certain family members or taking time for yourself when you need it. Boundaries are essential for maintaining your well-being. This is a huge and significant one for many. Often, our boundaries are tested and pushed. For whatever reason, our nature or our personality may fall into the trap of allowing the boundaries to be extended beyond our comfort zone, which can then lead to painful experiences.

9. **Building Resilience:** Resilience is the ability to bounce back from adversity. Building resilience involves developing healthy coping strategies, such as practicing mindfulness, engaging in physical activity, and maintaining a positive outlook.

10. **Creating New Connections:** As you heal, forming new relationships and redefining existing ones can help rebuild a sense of family. This might involve blending families, forming new friendships, or strengthening extended family ties.

11. **Embracing Possibilities:** Viewing brokenness as an opportunity for growth allows you to ask, "What else is possible?" This mindset encourages a forward-looking approach, focusing on potential and opportunity rather than just loss.

12. **Finding Joy:** Amidst the pain and loss, it's important to find moments of joy. Engage in activities that bring you happiness and fulfillment. This might involve spending time with loved ones, pursuing a hobby, or simply taking time to relax and enjoy life. There is joy all around us and in us. Let it be what leads your day and guides you in each of life's choices.

The Journey to a Renewed Family

While the experience of a "broken family" can be profoundly challenging, it also offers the chance for profound growth and renewal. By redefining what family means and embracing the changes that come, individuals can find strength and new connections. Ultimately creating a family that, while different, can be just as meaningful and supportive.

The journey from brokenness to a renewed sense of family is deeply personal and unique to everyone. It requires a willingness to embrace change and to step into the unknown. The invitation to move forward is always present, and taking those steps, however small, can lead to a new and unbroken territory filled with potential and hope.

As we navigate the complexities of family life, it's important to remember that family is not defined by its structure, but by the love, support, and connections that bind us. No matter how broken a family might feel, there is always the potential for healing, growth, and renewal. Embrace the journey and find strength in the bonds that remain and the new ones that form along the way. Divorce doesn't define you unless you allow it to. Divorce means something was very broken and unable to be repaired. It takes strength to identify this and to recognize that being together is worse for the relationship and the children than going your separate ways.

I have learned that we can never really know how life will turn out. We have our intentions and plans, or so we think, but sometimes they change. Being a single mom with two incredible boys, I knew that I had to find the way to heal, to embrace each day, and to never give up. They needed me and I needed them. Through this lens of strength, our family prevailed. We are all in healthy relationships and I have remarried; happy ever after really does exist. Embracing the gift of each day filled with gratitude will serve you and those around you in a positive and impactful way.

Erica Bearss

Erica Bearss first pursued excellence in sports. She won two gold medals in the Ontario Provincial Ringette, played Varsity Field Hockey, competed in AAA ice hockey for BC, and was part of Team Canada in the ITU World Triathlon Grand Final in London, UK. Alongside her athletic career, Erica advocates for education. She completed a BA with Honours in Modern Languages and Literature and an MBA in Leadership and Management. After years of industry experience, she is now educating at universities and technical colleges across North America.

Erica has held several leadership and consulting roles in a variety of industries. She also has a passion for acting. Her participation in community theatre complements regular appearances on stage, in commercials and short films. A natural adventurer and leader, Erica is an avid traveller and is fluent in English, French and Spanish.

Most importantly, Erica is a dedicated mother to two bright and inspiring young boys who are already developing into athletes and adventurers themselves. Together, they continue to seek new challenges and discover new opportunities. Erica lives and works with a mindset of collaboration, innovation, and excellence.

Connect with Erica:
https://linktr.ee/ericabearss

Chapter 3

Bootcamp For Your Brain!

By Erica Bearss

I am awesome. I can and, I will.

This chapter is going to begin with the end in mind. I would like you to use your voice and mind to say, "I am awesome, I can and, I will." Do this at least 5 to 10 times right now, aloud, if possible, and with purpose.

I am 100% okay if you already think I am bizarre. As Aristotle said, "No great mind has ever existed without a touch of madness." Being a little "crazy" has made me the success I am today. I can assure you that I have a massive heart with lots of love and support to give. I practice both transformational and servant leadership intending to make the world a better place. For now, my focus is on family, workplace environments and the next generation.

When I started writing this chapter, I asked myself: What do I want to teach my little boys (who are 5 and 7 at the time of writing this) as they grow up, so they can live their best lives?

One of my favourite quotes I use as a pillar in my life and share often is by Sun-Tzu: "In the midst of chaos, there is also opportunity." I live knowing these outlooks to be true.

Life is a roller coaster and will *not* always be easy. It is what we do with (or how we process) whatever comes at us that matters most. In my experience, we can navigate our emotions to spectacular places. I plan to share with you and future generations how I learned to overcome huge obstacles and challenges by treating my brain as a muscle and focusing on living my best life. I will share how I found opportunity in chaos, how I exercise my brain, and how I continue to learn to use my voice for good.

Obstacles I have personally faced include but are not limited to sexual abuse, heartbreak, a near-death car accident that caused a severe brain injury (read my chapter in *Let's Not Sugar Coat It*), a ruptured placenta during childbirth, bullying at the workplace (read my chapter in *Culture Revolution: 13 Insights for Organizational Culture*), and the death of a parent (my Dad—my rock).

I want to emphasize to readers that I am not a victim. Everyone in the world faces challenges and we are all on different journeys. We all have our story and have experienced trauma of some kind. Your story is just as important as mine. I intend to share how I overcame and persevered and to provide insights into lessons I have learned later in life, that I wish I had known before. I want to show you that you **can** overcome any obstacle and live your best life.

Have you ever walked away from a situation and said, "I wish I had said this" or "I wish I had done that"? I hope what I'm about to share can support or prevent prolonged hurt for the younger and future generations. As an educator at universities, technical colleges, and organizations across the globe, I am dedicated to supporting future generations to live their best lives.

Lesson 1: Use your voice and speak up!

I was sexually abused for years as a young girl. It took more than 10 years to overcome the abuse and understand that my body was not the only reason a man would like me and that it was okay for me to enjoy sexual interactions. I later found out that the same man abused a friend of mine. I wish I had spoken up sooner! I wish I had told my

Mum or Dad that our neighbour was sexually abusing me when he came over. If I had said something, it would have helped other women, and I would have had healthier relationships with men. Sadly, there were few role models back then leading the way and as 6–10-year-olds, we are not equipped to understand the severity of sexual abuse. This happened in the '80s, long before "#metoo" and other social movements around abuse came to light.

Thank God for my mother. These experiences had been impacting my behavior in my tween and teen years, and she noticed. One day, she came home with a bottle of "bubbles" (sparkling wine), sat me down and said, "We need to talk." Everything finally came out. I spoke up for the first time. A huge weight was lifted from my shoulders. It was like the clouds cleared. To this day, I drink bubbles because they make me feel euphoric on so many levels. The memory of that day was transformational. Most importantly, this is when I started to grow stronger.

Even though my battle to rebuild trust continued to spill into work, life, and relationships/interactions with men working in male-dominated sectors, I had learned how to use my voice. There were times when my body was used to make deals, get promotions, and influence business decisions because a part of me still thought that was right. It was not right. It is not right. Thankfully, the journey that began with my mother's intervention bore fruit, and, in time, my voice grew louder. I built the strength to discover the power to change my story. In less than five years, I achieved VP-level positions at multiple companies, was asked to join numerous corporate boards of directors, and ultimately started my own consulting business that has successfully attracted many clients. Not only was my voice heard but I became a leader. More importantly, I learned that I did not have to do it all on my own. After speaking out, a village formed around me. Find and build your village, support and care for them, and they will do the same for you.

Remember, our body is ours and we decide what is best for it. Your body includes your mind. If you are a person being abused in any way, please speak up. Please find your power. By speaking up, you can shorten a long battle overcoming trauma and help future potential targets before it is too late. I will continuously advocate for the movement to raise awareness against violence against women. #metoo #OrangeTheWorld #TimesUp

Lesson 2: Play Sports and think of your brain as a muscle (make it part of your exercise routine)

The brain is an organ; many studies prove exercising the brain can support a healthier and potentially longer life.

Another key phrase I live by is, "Stay social and stay active." Sports have saved me at numerous stages in my life. My parents put us into every sport available. This kept us active and social and gave us a competitive edge. As a young girl, our team won two gold provincial championship medals in ringette. I also played hockey for hours at the local outdoor rinks in Ottawa, was the only girl on the boys' baseball team, and won multiple trophies and ribbons in karate and swimming.

As a tween and teen, we moved into a high school for grades 7 and 8. The effects of my sexual abuse came to a head as older boys and talks of sex came into the picture. Navigating hormones hit hard. I started hanging out with a rough crowd and encountered my first real experiences with bullies. It was a very challenging and dark time in my life journey. Thankfully, my number one fans (family) supported a move to a school that focused more on sports. The lessons I learned set me up for success in the new school. I knew exactly where to focus. Sports! I joined the field hockey and rugby teams and became captain of both. By the time I was in grade 11, I played on the A teams and coached the B teams. Sports kept me focused and helped me let out my frustrations, make lifetime friendships, and learn how to strategize, collaborate, and lead. It also got me a spot on the varsity field hockey team at Ottawa University.

Those provincial ringette gold medals and countless hours at the outdoor rinks landed me a spot on the AAA women's hockey team in British Columbia, which kept me fit and focused for years, as well as built lifetime friendships. Following my hockey career, I started running marathons and competing in triathlons. My goal became to complete an Ironman, which I accomplished in Thailand in 2012.

I had a life-changing experience after my Ironman in Thailand. On the way to the airport, the taxi driver fell asleep at the wheel, and we crashed into a concrete wall. I went through the windshield and was unconscious. All my ribs were broken, my thorax was crushed, and my head and face were sliced by glass and crushed on impact. In addition to the physical effects, I had what the doctors called a severe brain injury (aka TBI). When I was accompanied home after 10 days in the hospital in Thailand, I could not even write an email. I had lost memories, cognitive skills and motor skills. How would I ever overcome this? In all transparency, I did not think I would. I went to a dark place and thought the world would be better without me and perhaps I could not go on. So, what did I do? I decided to **"exercise my brain."** I recalled winning a spot to compete in my age group for a sprint triathlon in the ITU grand final in London, UK. How would I get back to where I was in my athletic ability? I needed a plan. Thankfully, because I was in the best shape of my life (physically) at the time of the accident, my body healed quickly. I worked with nurses on my brain and hired the most incredible coach on earth, Ken Hamilton, to bring me back to life in triathlons. We started at 10 minutes a day. I raced in that triathlon, and it brought me back to life. It gave me purpose. I went from broken and bruised to tears of joy from accomplishing something I did not think I could do. Exercising our brain is critical and when we do it, we can accomplish the impossible. I wrote goals and self-affirmations everywhere to convince my brain (me) that I could do it. I am living proof that you can change your mind by exercising your brain and body through pain or roadblocks. Another saying I live by is: "Mind over matter." If you are interested in the framework I built to exercise my brain, check out my chapter in the book called *Let's Not Sugar Coat It!* Reset, Realize, Reframe, Recommit! Remember, you are awesome, you can, and you will!

Lesson 3: Listen to your gut and find your culture club

More recently, I worked in a toxic work environment. A great leader left halfway through my contract. They were empowering and valued the idea of an ethical corporate culture. At this point, I considered leaving too but didn't listen to my instincts. A new person was appointed (internally) to try and fill the gap. Unfortunately, this person was sexist, racist, and unprofessional on many levels. Not the ethical leader I was accustomed to. During a meeting, the newly appointed leader stated they needed to fire the cleaning person. When asked why, they responded, "They are too hot, and I cannot concentrate when they come into my office." Given my experience in male-dominant workplaces and the fact that I advocate for diversity, respect, equity, equality and inclusion, this was completely inappropriate. Taken aback, I simply responded "You can't say those kinds of things. It's sexist and unprofessional." They replied, "It was a joke" and laughed. This was a PG example and only one of many sexist and inappropriate comments from this person. I desperately wanted to speak up; however, the HR person at this workplace was hired around the same time and was equally unprofessional. My gut was getting louder and shouting at me to quickly exit this culture. I was not in a position, nor did I have the capacity, to take on a deep-rooted toxic culture. My instincts were fighting with my loyal work ethic, and I had built a successful team in my department, which made this decision challenging. As I worked with this tummy ache, I kept seeing incredibly valuable and ethical employees leaving the company. This observation made my gut shout! I made one more attempt towards a lateral move in the organization in hopes of hiding from the daily interactions with a toxic culture but was again faced with more discomfort. I learned the company practiced nepotism and unfair hiring practices. At this point, my dedication, loyalty and trust were lost, and I disengaged completely from the work. I exited the organization, and it was the best business result imaginable. A massive weight was lifted from my mind and body; the daily challenges of a toxic work culture were eliminated. New doors of opportunity were opened that I could finally see. I missed these doors when I was stuck in the dark clouds of a toxic work culture. It ignited my career as an author, speaker, and advocate for social justice. I am living proof that when you close a chapter that is destroying your soul, new, empowering and exciting chapters open! Listen to your gut! I wish I had listened sooner! As Milton Berle would say, "If opportunity doesn't knock, build a door."

The day I listened and built a door in my mind, my life became infinitely better. In addition to the new opportunities, I realized that speaking up for myself was not enough—I wanted to speak up for others as well. This sparked my dedication over the next decade to advocate and educate about strong ethical corporate cultures. One important success was writing a chapter in a book called *Culture Revolution: 13 Insights for Organizational Culture*. This is a movement supporting companies looking to build strong ethical corporate cultures where employees feel safe to speak up, companies build strong core and ethical values, and employees are dedicated and enjoy their work environment. I continue to teach Business Ethics, Change Management, and Organizational Behavior at Universities across North America. Building ethical corporate cultures is a predominant focus in every course I teach. We need to ensure there are safe spaces for people to speak up. I encourage you to join me in being that person, being that company, or advocating for ethical leaders and safe spaces.

There is a plethora of lessons to learn in life and so many I would have loved to share in detail. Prioritizing the ones I felt most important was an accepted challenge. I have shared above the top three (in no particular order). Below are two mini lessons that would support a balanced approach to a life beyond what you think is possible!

Lesson 4: Travel is the best education

Make it a priority in life to see the world. It has been the greatest education of my life. I am an advocate for getting an education but travelling will expand your mind and knowledge in the best ways possible. Live and breathe other cultures and places. Learn a new language. Listen to international music. Eat food from across the globe. Embrace diversity and understand different ways of life. Expand the frames of your mind! I think I am one of the luckiest people on earth to have been to as many places across the world as I have. I also know that I made it happen because I made it a priority. Ever since I was little, we travelled. With a Canadian diplomat as a father and a Scottish mother raised in Australia, it was part of our life. When I was 15, I vowed to go somewhere I had never been to every year of my life. Travelling, learning cultures, and seeing different places expand our global mindset. This helps us with our ability to communicate, to understand and embrace new perspectives. It is a fundamental part of my brain exercise routine.

Lesson 5: Learn the triple bottom line (keys to sustainability) in this order: People>Planet>Profit!

Your village is critical and the environment you have or build around you is fundamental. If you build your village and the environment you want, the profit will follow. I recall in my earlier career days that money was the most important thing when it came to working. I always hoped for fulfillment, but money mattered more. Now that I am working in a fulfilling industry with many amazing people and making a profit, I realize that doing what you love matters. If you focus and plan it right, you can find sustainability.

"I am awesome. I can and, I will." This simple mantra can carry you through some of the toughest times in life. Why? Because it trains your brain to see the positive light in dark situations. Do you know that gut feeling that kicks in when you face a challenge? That is your mind's way of communicating with you. When we regularly use these mantras or phrases (like the ones I've shared), we teach our brains to recognize our strength and wisdom. We all have these tools within us; we simply need to learn how to tap into them. On a physiological level, have you ever noticed that the physical feelings of "nervousness" and "excitement" have an incredibly similar sensation? Imagine a world where we can guide our nerves into excitement; the outcomes become exponentially different. Music can also connect and help guide our physical to mental pathways, so I would like to leave you with a mood-changing anthem by Jason Mraz. Search for the song, "Look for the Good" and listen to the lyrics. I hope that by sharing how I have conquered the bumps in the road of my life, you will discover how to navigate any obstacle that comes across your path.

To answer my earlier question and the focus of this chapter, I dedicate this work to my two incredible boys, who will be leaders in our future. I will strive daily to give them the tools they need to be strong, safe and confident and live their best lives.

Heather Andrews

Heather Andrews is a dynamic speaker, 14-time best-selling Amazon author, and successful publisher. She empowers individuals to take control of their narratives, having guided over 400 authors to share their unique wisdom with the world. Through her company, she has published 45 books, with 26 achieving #1 bestseller status.

Raised in rural Alberta, Heather's sense of community has been a guiding principle throughout her life. With a 34-year career in Healthcare—spanning X-ray Technology, Management, and Strategic Leadership—her work has taken her across borders, deepening her understanding of diverse perspectives and stories. This global exposure fuels her passion for connecting with people on a heart level.

Believing in a new era of Women Empowerment through collaboration and connection, Heather serves on the Advisory Board of Directors for **Twenty-Seven Degrees**, driving global visibility for women entrepreneurs through lifestyle magazine profiles and authentic storytelling. Her mission is to foster relationships that inspire business empowerment, influence, and impact. By helping women harness the power of their stories, she enables them to be seen, heard, and understood, all while generating and leveraging new income streams.

Connect with Heather:

https://linktr.ee/heatherlandrews

Chapter 4

Let Love Lead You

By Heather Andrews

When you love yourself, love will find you.

I looked into his eyes as he stood in the kitchen. Darius Rucker's song, "So I Sang" played in the background. My handsome Viking partner came out from behind the counter as he was cooking, and I knew he wanted to dance with me. Kitchen dancing, who knew it was a thing? "I can't dance," I told myself. "He will judge me." My ex-husband never danced with me because I stepped on his toes several times. I knew dancing with a partner was never in the cards for me. I was tone-deaf.

My partner was coming closer to me and looked into my eyes. It was as hot as a steamy romance novel. He did not speak but only gazed at me. We stood three feet apart and he pointed to his foot tapping. I did the same. I was feeling the music and tapping in sync with him. He moved closer to me, put his hand on my hip and I went to put my hand on his shoulder; he shook his head, No.

He started to move, and I moved with him. I could feel the music. Was it perfect? Absolutely not. But I was dancing with a partner, MY partner. The tears rolled down my cheeks as I found a new way to learn as he taught me. I found a new belief. I trusted myself to move with him and surrender to his leading. Not only was this a dance move, but it was also a level of trust with intimacy that I had never experienced with a man.

Over the next few months, we kitchen danced; and by the time the Calgary Stampede came to town, we were out dancing at a Western bar. We were the only ones on the dance floor and we two stepped in sync, dancing to "Dust On The Bottle" by David Lee Murphy. My friend took a video of us. When she sent it to me, I reflected on all the years I stayed stuck in a belief that I could not dance. The lesson I've learned is that I can change my story if I am willing to trust change.

I shared this story in a keynote speech in 2024 in front of 200 women. My partner, who did not know how much dancing with him impacted me, was also there. One of the audience members mentioned he may have had a tear or two roll down his cheek.

This story goes deeper than just dancing in the kitchen.

At the ripe age of 53, I met someone who taught me what true intimacy was, how to be a partner in a relationship, and how to be open to being loved and receiving that love.

My best friend introduced us, but it was a business introduction. Who knew it would turn into a beautiful loving relationship? I have been married twice before; the first one ended in divorce when I was 23 and the second one ended after 28 years together and three amazing kids. The reason for leaving these marriages: neither man filled my soul anymore.

I fought for my second marriage but soon realized that it couldn't be a one-way street. On my 49th birthday, my two oldest children came to me and said, "You and Dad aren't happy anymore. Please fix it." Those words rippled through my mind, and I explored my feelings and how I felt about this marriage. When my daughter left for university, I felt a piece of me die that day. It became clear to me that I felt so alone. My two sons were old enough to do their own thing and my ex-husband loved to game on his computer.

Some days, it felt like he had checked out of the marriage, or maybe I had. I reached out to counsellors and divorce lawyers—it took me three months to make a decision. Until one day, I looked my ex in the eyes and said, "I don't want to be married anymore." With a look of shock and horror, he tried to talk me out of it, but I was done. Within days, I felt bold enough to break the news to our children, who were 17, 19, and 22 at the time. Mama bear mode kicked in; I wanted to protect my kids and not have them scarred by the experience. I didn't want them to lose their home, and I didn't want to face a long legal battle. Because of my ex-husband's reaction, I stayed in the house to protect him against himself.

I made the mistake of choosing to leave with nothing. I walked away from our matrimonial home because I wanted my kids to still have a home. I did not want to fight. However, when the time came to do the paperwork, I took the debt, and he got the house. It was the dumbest thing I ever did but my heart and love for my family got in the way of my financial stability. This happened five years ago, and I am still recovering. I learned that I made that decision because I felt like I was not worthy of what I had worked so hard to build, even though I was entitled to half. My ex-husband has since remarried and moved out of the country, and my two sons now live in the home they grew up in.

Money comes and goes. Would I do things differently if I could go back? Yes, I would. However, I am grateful for the path I chose because, in today's economy, it is difficult for young adults to get financially ahead. My kids are safe, and they can work toward their future. What is most important to me is my relationship with my children, and my love for them motivated the decision I made.

So often we think we are doing what is right for everyone else, but I have come to realize that I am as important as everyone else in my life. The martyr theory has not worked so well for me. I believe this notion, that I had to sacrifice everything for the sake of others, stemmed from a young age as I watched my mom do everything for us. She was always strong, resilient, and very self-sacrificing. My mom loved us to her core, and still does, but she was always stoic and poised. Even when my dad died in a car accident, she shed tears for about a day then it was onward and upward. I tried to be this way during my divorce. But several years later, I think I cracked as we were in the thick of COVID-19 and had too much time to think.

I delved into the dating world looking for connection. I had moved in with my mom as she needed help due to a stroke she had earlier in 2019, right when I left my marriage. I asked a friend about online dating, and she explained the ins and outs of it. I created my profiles on Tinder and Bumble. I wondered if I would get any swipes as a twice-divorced 50-year-old woman. I read many profiles of men because I found it fascinating to see what they were looking for. What is FWB, sapiosexual, or vanilla? I felt like I was stepping into a new world.

I asked a friend of mine if it was too soon to be doing this and she said, "Let it be a path of discovery for you. Learn what you like and don't like. Sample the buffet, so to speak."

I found that entering the dating world again during a global pandemic was kind of perfect because it meant that I got to know people through phone calls and text messages. Once social distancing had been lifted, I met several men whom I had been speaking with which led to some short-term relationships. My perspective of online dating was that some think they want a relationship but don't, while others think FWB is a relationship, but it isn't. I did eventually meet someone and dated him for two years. He was kind, sweet, and fun, but the problem was he couldn't move on from his ex-wife. That relationship ended with me leaving his house at 2:30 in the morning and going back to my condo. I was grateful for the fact that I had a home of my own to return to.

My lessons from the dating world were:

- I am still attractive and desirable but do not need to give myself sexually to be accepted by a partner.
- I need to have my sense of self, stand in my power, and choose what's right for me before I can give myself wholly to someone else.
- Never go back to a past relationship; only move forward.

I have a tattoo on my forearm that says, "I am the creator of my story." This is my mantra for my life. I am a huge believer in picking the stories that will either propel us forward or hold us back. Having merged with a larger publishing company after nine years, I am accountable for playing a part in the decisions I make. I have always known that with every choice, there is a consequence.

When I two-stepped with my partner that night during the Calgary Stampede, all I could think of was how every moment, every tear, every heartbreak, every experience, every smile, and every act of forgiveness led us together to meet, to grow and create our synergy and step into a life of synchronicity.

Is life perfect? No, it's not. Have I changed? Yes, I have.

Being open to receiving his love, I learned to dive into my inner being.

When I started my business in 2015, it was strictly by default, and it just landed in my lap much like my current partner. When the universe clicks like that, saying yes is easy. It made me say yes to creating a publishing company, and it made me say yes to dancing in the kitchen with my partner. I do not want to live a day without him.

While my publishing company is heading in an exciting direction, getting to this point didn't come easy. The effects of COVID-19 meant losing a great deal of money and watching a team of 30 people dismantle. After the pandemic, I had to change the business model and utilize all the knowledge I had to help people navigate their way to self-publish their books. Pivoting was a game-changer, and I've learned valuable lessons. Build your business globally, locally, and online. Ensure your lead generation is in more than one platform. Make your clients self-sufficient.

I've considered shutting down many times, but people kept showing interest in working with me and I knew I had to keep going. When times are tough, we need to bounce back and figure it out. Nothing is permanent and eventually, things do get better.

The duality of living in the present and working toward what you want is like walking a double-edged sword. Which edge do I walk on knowing I have lessons to learn while I am growing? I try to keep a positive mindset of abundance, knowing the powers of my resilience and growth are strengthening me while I am financially and emotionally bereft.

My "why" for wanting to keep my company is deeply anchored in me. I love helping women dive into their stories and watch their transformation. It is a deep-rooted passion, and I believe that the impact of their stories will inspire others.

As I walked through my divorce, my caretaking years with my mom, my leaving home with nothing more than my clothes since I left all the things I held most dear for my kids and their home, I knew it was all for a larger cause. My self-worth was in the gutter, but my empty soul screamed it was worth it.

Moving through the dating years, saving my company, and modelling the way for my kids to not stay in unhealthy relationships, I was finding myself. I was figuring out what I desired and what made me happy.

When I finally made my list for my business, my partner, and my life, everything slowly changed. I moved my mom into a condo community while I bought my own place. I manifested a like-minded man who understands business and the power of being an author because he, too, is published. He sees my vision. The funniest part is I always wanted to be in business with a life partner and I am happy to say that I have merged my publishing company with his, allowing us to create a business in which both of us will grow. It brings about a bigger vision. We are launching a company for women so they can have a space to be empowered and uplevel them on a global scale. Needless to say, I am so excited.

I remember the day we met; he was a client and then later became my boyfriend. The day I fell in love with him was the day he said, "You are a self-made woman, despite your trials and tribulations. You walk with victory." I knew at that moment that he was made for me. Since being with him, I have lost 40 lbs—he cooks and leads my workouts. My life changed once I surrendered to his kindness and found the strength to receive his love.

Abundance happened the moment I stopped resisting the idea of joining him in business and trusting the process. I still have to take drastic action to grow what we are creating; but now, I am not doing it alone. Although, I was never really alone. I've always had my tribe who believed in me, supported my business, and referred me to others.

When I stood on stage and told the kitchen dance story for the second time, people came to me and said the more they heard that story, the more they could relate to shifting their story.

As I reflect on these hard times, I realize that they were rewarding, and it was all uncharted territory. Upon discovering that this path was meant to form my vision, I leaned in and listened to the universe like I never had before.

I am the creator of my story and so darn excited to share my lessons with the world, so that our younger women can walk their journey with a new enlightened perspective. Keep your eyes wide open on your dreams despite the rough road that occurs. The life you desire is within reach.

Jackie McCoy

Jackie McCoy is an Edmonton-based engineer, mentor, and rugby coach. With a passion for continuous improvement, Jackie thrives in her engineering career, where she excels at solving complex problems while mentoring engineers at all stages of their careers. Her dedication to fostering growth and learning drives her to help others reach their full potential in the workplace.

A proud mother of two beautiful daughters, Jackie finds inspiration in balancing her career and family life. She strives to be a role model for her children, teaching them the importance of resilience, hard work, and self-improvement through her actions at home and in her professional life. As her daughters have taken up rugby, she has reignited her own passion for the sport. A former competitive rugby player, Jackie returned to the field as a coach, now sharing the values of teamwork, discipline, and self-belief with young athletes.

In addition to her engineering and coaching roles, Jackie serves as the director of the McCoy Family Foundation, which funds youth's educational journeys. Through the foundation, she ensures that young people have the resources they need to pursue their academic dreams and succeed in life, reflecting her belief in the power of education and opportunity.

As a first-time author, Jackie draws on her diverse experiences to tell stories of resilience, growth, and the importance of lifelong learning, all of which reflect her commitment to continuous self-improvement and empowering others.

Connect with Jackie:

https://linktr.ee/jackiemccoy?utm_source=linktree_admin_share

Chapter 5

Perfection Isn't the Damn Goal

By Jackie McCoy

If I could impart to you one thing, it would be this... Perfection is NOT your damn goal. Your focus should only be on IMPROVEMENT. Perfection leads to judgment, stifles progress, and limits dreams. However, focusing on continuous improvement creates a willingness to be coached, allows acceptance of feedback, opens the door to self-awareness, creates self-acceptance, and challenges dreams to evolve slowly.

Being told from an early age that I wasn't perfect most likely made it easier for me to overcome the perfection hurdles plaguing most overachievers. I was in grade 2 when my teachers figured out that I hadn't learned to read because I was both cross-eyed and had a learning disability. Having the world think I was dumb was probably my greatest blessing. My natural coping mechanism had me mastering my learning style quickly. I learned by paying attention to everything that was said in class and asking many clarifying questions (because one thing I was never going to do was go back to the chapter or my notes to read the instructions). Being willing to say, "I don't understand" helped me more than the times it hurt me when people judged me for being stupid. I was so far from being perfect that perfection was never my goal. On top of that, the world gave me so much praise for just getting better, that getting better every day has become a long-standing habit.

I still succumbed to the need to be perfect, but when it was coupled with comparison, and it was the absolute worst. Those junior high days (specifically grade 8) were socially the hardest years of my life. I compared myself to everyone and would look for ways that I was better than literally everyone in my life. If you were prettier than me, I was going to prove to myself that I was smarter. If you were smarter, I would have more friends; if you had the same friends as me, I would be better friends with my best friend than you were. It was exhausting. This never-ending game of comparison had me in the worst mindset, which ultimately meant I never won. I didn't use those comparisons to motivate myself to be better or improve. This toxic thinking pattern only hurt me. I was probably the meanest person I have ever known. I didn't like who I was, and things needed to change.

    I found that team sports were a fantastic way to receive positive affirmations, and it was rugby that ended my toxic comparison trait. By the nature of the sport, rugby requires all different body types and athletic skills. The team celebrates when the big and tall girls catch the ball in the line out or when the small and fast girls score a try on the outside, and everyone gets pumped when anyone makes a hard tackle. The point is that there is no perfect body for rugby. The team succeeds when everyone on the team feels powerful and that only happens when each member is celebrated for what they bring to the team.

    My eyes were opened to a unique way of living and thinking when I learned the value of diversity in friendships. My new group of friends were happy about my success without comparison to themselves and became a safe place for me when things didn't go as planned. These friends were accepting of people and helped me become more content with just being me. I still run into people who have a comparison mindset or at least people who bring out that past habit in me. I could feel this slowly dim my light. As I matured, I started to make decisions to limit time with those people.

Anyone who has played with or against me in any of my sporting endeavors would definitely say that I'm competitive and aggressive. Out of all the sports and teams I've played in, and even with all the awards I've won, I was never the BEST nor perfect. I can attribute all my athletic success to my willingness to work hard to get better in every game. I played on the University of Alberta (U of A) Pandas rugby team for the first two years of their existence. We dominated the varsity league right from the first game we ever played. Being the best wasn't the goal of the Pandas rugby team; the goal was to constantly get better. This led the team to six straight national championships, resulting in us getting inducted into the U of A Hall of Fame.

Can you believe that my first rugby coaches almost wrote me off? I missed the first two high school rugby games because I had to work. In the third game (of a very short season), I reminded them that they hadn't put me in yet. The coaches just shrugged and said it was too late for me to figure out how to play the sport. Since there was no pressure to be the best, I was free to just try it out. When they subbed me in at the next kickoff, I caught the ball and ran it into the endzone for my first try (that's like a touchdown in football). I didn't allow the fear of not knowing what to do or being bad at rugby to stop me from trying. Playing rugby was the best life-changing decision I ever made.

If you aren't spending energy trying to convince people that you are perfect (or smart), you have more time to actually learn. This couldn't have been truer than in my first year of engineering (yup, it turns out I wasn't as dumb as people thought). I'm convinced the first year wasn't as hard for me as my fellow students, and that was for one reason—I was well-trained in asking questions, telling people I didn't understand, and that I needed more help. Other engineering students would spend hours on one question, reading and rereading their notes and the textbooks, trying to figure it out for themselves. If I couldn't answer it myself in 15 minutes, I started asking questions. I would walk through CAB (the geeky part of the University of Alberta campus where all the first-year engineers worked on assignments), go up to different tables, and just ask questions. I'd teach people the questions I knew, and in exchange, they'd help me with the questions I didn't. If there were questions no one knew, then I'd head straight to the professor or TA to be taught the answers. I saved myself hours of homework and I'd know all the material because I taught multiple people the answers to the questions. Did many of those engineers judge me for being dumb? Yes, they did. Again, my goal wasn't perfection, and it wasn't to be the smartest engineer in the room. My goal was to learn, which meant putting myself out there (without self-judgment) and advocating for my learning style. My other goal was to complete my engineering work as fast as possible so I could enjoy other aspects of university life.

With school and rugby behind me, my next chapter brought marriage, motherhood, and an engineering career. Many working moms worry about not being a good mother and I wasn't immune. I'm a mother of two wonderful daughters. Right from the start of motherhood, it was clear I was far from perfect. Trying to be the perfect mom just isn't possible. I was the mom who had a diaper bag without diapers. I was also the mom who would tell others about my "mom fails" so I could get their tips on how to do things better.

I remember watching the movie *Bad Moms* and resonating with so many scenes. The one thing that changed after watching that movie was that I stopped referring to myself as a "bad mom" to my friends. I was a great mom doing my best even when I made mistakes along the way. I definitely ran into those moms who wanted or needed to be viewed as perfect. But the way I generated my mom friends was through authentic connections about how being a mother was hard and filled with plenty of situations in which to learn. I nearly peed myself during the one scene in the movie when the mom was rushing to get to school pick up so she could get her kids to their after-school activities. When the kids were in the car, the mom told them that she was doing her best and the kid, with a look of sheer disappointment, said, "I know."

My kids hated being late to anything and would prefer not to go at all than to walk in late. This became a major stressor for me as a working single mom of two highly active girls. I did everything I could to get out of work on time, but there was always someone who would keep me in the office 10 minutes more than I wanted. The entire time I drove through traffic, I would be filled with dread about what my kids would say to me, praying for no red lights, and trying to beat the school bell. Even on days I would make it on time, I would still beat myself up during the drive there because I had this story of being a bad mom in my head.

At one point, the stress was so much that I set up a plan to be transparent with everyone at work. I scheduled my departure time in my work calendar. I told my team and my leaders the days I needed to leave. I even had an official alternative work arrangement approved by my leader and HR. So, when people came up to talk to me, I had the confidence to say I needed to leave at a specific time and my coworkers were incredibly supportive and understanding. I was trying to be a perfect employee and coworker by staying later than I wanted, but really, I was a better employee and leader when I was transparent about my commitment to my children. I was able to follow up with them when I had the proper time to commit to the conversation and resolve their issue more directly.

Dealing with work wasn't the only key to relieving this stress. I needed to have an honest conversation with my girls. I sat them down and told them I was doing my absolute best. I was honest with them, and they were honest back. One of them said, "But your best isn't good enough," which felt like a knife to the heart. However, it was a great transition into an open conversation that our best is ALWAYS good enough. That doesn't mean we can't figure out how to be better in the future, but for today, my best is always good enough.

When you are not trying to put out a facade of perfection, it is easier to show up authentically to others and allow them to support you in tough times. I raised my daughters to believe they were destined to be great but found that I was unintentionally driving perfectionism. I needed to be intentional in communicating that being great isn't about being perfect. Instead, it is about getting better every day and that mistakes are just as acceptable as successes.

I believe in leading by example—by showing them that trying your best and learning from your mistakes is a better measure of hard work. I believe the trick to really teaching them this lesson is being honest and transparent when I fail. My kids hear my stories of failure all the time. Sometimes they are funny stories where I made a fool of myself at the grocery store. Sometimes they are minor parenting failures where I needed to apologize for a forgotten permission form or a missed hot lunch order. Sometimes they are co-parenting fails and I needed to own up to not properly keeping their dad in the loop of something important. Sometimes they are even bigger failures. When I was laid off from a wonderful company, it was hard not to feel ashamed. I told my oldest daughter first and her response was, "It's their loss and I'm not worried that you'll get a great new job." Then I told my youngest daughter and her response was, "So, what's going to be our next wonderful job?" She said, "our job" and it hit me that she's on my team no matter what company chooses to employ me. When they fail, I don't allow shame to creep into the conversation. So when I felt I'd failed at something I have been so successful at for so many years, they didn't allow me to feel one moment of shame.

Despite being laid off, I have still been highly successful in my 20 years working for large corporations. When I first started, one of the jokes in the control room was that junior engineers would walk in and say, "Hi, I'm an engineer. How can I help you?" Any team, project, or initiative that anyone joins is usually because they want to help. However, what you think is helpful or needed might not be what is actually needed. Your first goal should be to listen, ask questions, and consume the whole problem. The best place to start is assuming that you or your team aren't perfect, and your goal ought to be finding out how you and your team can get better. When people see changes based on the feedback they have been given, they will be more willing to alter their own behaviors, processes, or work outcomes based on others' feedback as well. I won't bother you with complex work stories of increase in production, reduction of expenses, or alteration of company culture, but the value of opening yourself up to feedback so that you can be self-aware is priceless and necessary for continuous improvement in all areas of your work and home life.

Another large failure in my life was the breakdown of my almost 10-year marriage. The drama and gossip that goes with an unexpected marriage breakdown can be overwhelming. In the months after our separation, the stories shared by parties outside my ex and myself, the inappropriate questions asked by acquaintances, and the outside judgment were hard for me to consume because I felt so ashamed. I found the way to process the separation was to eliminate the shame I felt surrounding the break-up. Instead of being defensive or claiming the higher ground because I didn't do anything wrong, I reflected deeply to see how I could have contributed to the relationship breakdown. When I was able to see my part without shame, I was able to control my next steps and set myself and my girls up for a positive future. My ex and I still have co-parenting issues, but eliminating the shame allowed me to show up in our new relationship as a level-headed parent who consistently makes decisions that are in the best interest of the children and not my ego. My resilience to my marriage breakdown has allowed me and my girls to live a happy life with their dad in the picture.

Perfectionism, coupled with a comparison mindset, can be mentally draining for Type A overachievers like me. However, looking back at my life, my greatest successes and my best friendships were made when I was authentically myself and willing to expose my flaws. My resilience to negative life events was always made easier when I took shame out of the equation. Even though it's hard, when I can objectively see my flaws, I can process and recover from setbacks. My hope for everyone is that you can take being perfect off the table. The longer you can live in a situation where you are the one learning and growing, the more you will be able to accomplish and rebound faster than you originally thought possible. So instead of perfection, I challenge you to commit to only getting better every day.

Jennifer Gordon

Jennifer Gordon is a breast cancer survivor and advocate whose journey is one of resilience, self-love, and empowerment. Diagnosed during the chaos of the COVID-19 pandemic, she faced her battle head-on, combining a double mastectomy with reconstruction in a single 15-hour surgery. Alongside her healing, Jennifer embarked on a transformative path, exploring tantra and sexual wellness, and discovering the power of pleasure and self-care in recovery. As a confidence and sexual wellness coach, she's passionate about helping others reconnect with their bodies, and treat them as beloved companions.

Jennifer is also an accomplished dragon boater who has won numerous gold medals, finding strength in the camaraderie of fellow survivors. Her journey from the depths of trauma to a place of profound self-respect and joy inspires others to embrace their own healing with courage and humor.

Connect with Jennifer:

https://linktr.ee/TheBlissPoint

Chapter 6

A Survivor's Journey Through Self-Love and Healing

By Jennifer Gordon

It was November 2020, and the world was deep in the throes of the COVID-19 pandemic. I was packing up my desk to work from home when I noticed a mammogram requisition pinned to my bulletin board. I'm a procrastinator's procrastinator and that little slip of paper had been there for two years. My ADHD brain knew that if I packed it away in my briefcase, it would disappear into the void, like a sock in the dryer. So, instead of ignoring it for another day, I did something out of character—I booked the appointment right then and there, expecting it might take a year to get in due to the pandemic. But the universe had other plans. There was a cancellation, and within four days, I found myself going for a biopsy. Four days after that, I was diagnosed with breast cancer.

To say that week was a whirlwind would be an understatement. I signed my separation papers, COVID-19 lockdown 2.0 hit, and I was handed a cancer diagnosis all at once. The stress was monumental—more than I ever imagined I could endure. But humans are resilient, aren't we? We push through, even when it feels impossible. My medical team and I quickly devised a surgical plan. Given the state of the world, I was terrified of being in the hospital while immune-compromised, risking exposure to COVID-19. However, I couldn't bear the thought of putting my family members at risk by having them shuttle me to and from treatment. So, I decided to take cancer down in one blow—a double mastectomy and reconstruction, all in one 15-hour surgery.

Never in my life had I experienced so much physical and emotional pain simultaneously. It felt as though a chunk had been torn from my body, and the surgeons somehow pieced me back together. Even though my new breasts were made from my own abdominal tissue, they didn't feel like mine. I was constantly afraid they would crack like glass, or that they'd fall off my body like something out of a cartoon. It took months before I felt safe walking around, unafraid of bumping into something and experiencing unbearable pain.

To truly understand the depth of this experience, let me rewind a bit. Back in 2019, I was studying Tantra and sexuality in a last-ditch effort to save my failing marriage. I had also begun a bariatric weight loss program, tipping the scales at 350 pounds. Food has always been my refuge, the only place I allowed myself joy. But as I started to confront my food addiction, I realized I needed to find other sources of joy. That's when my journey with Tantra truly began. At the age of 45, I started to discover all the different ways my body could experience pleasure—ways I had never known before. The most surprising discovery was that I could orgasm through nipple stimulation. This revelation came just six months before my cancer diagnosis, and I was furious. It felt like I was about to lose two extra clitorises.

Determined not to let cancer rob me of my newfound sensuality, I began a daily ritual of Tantric breast massages in the 30 days leading up to my surgery. Every morning and evening, I would talk to my breasts, thanking them, telling them how beautiful they were, and soaking up all the joy they could give me. Then, I'd rub my abdominal area—the tissue that would soon become my new breasts—and tell it to remember the pleasure, to remember that this was going to be its new job. My goal was to teach my neuropathways an alternate route to breast pleasure, even without nipples.

A part of me was consumed with self-pity during this time. I was newly single and living in isolation because of COVID-19. I couldn't risk being intimate with anyone for fear of jeopardizing my surgery if I got sick. That's when I realized I had to become my own epic lover. I had to take responsibility for my own pleasure and be my own partner; so began my love affair with my breasts. Every morning, I'd start with my breast massage, followed by meditation. Then, I would schedule grief time—I'd cry, sometimes on camera, so that I wouldn't feel alone. I'd even watch the videos back and cry some more, so I felt like I was crying with someone. To ensure my mood rebounded from these depths of despair, I'd put on my favorite dance videos and dance. On weekends, I dressed up, put on high heels and makeup, and hung up a disco ball, then danced all night as if I were at the bar. It was as if I was playing with myself— breast cancer Barbie in full swing.

One of the most transformative experiences during this time was a "Bye-Bye Booby" boudoir shoot. A photographer came and captured my original breasts in a series of intimate, emotional photos. By then, I had lost about 125 pounds, and seeing my transformed body in these portraits was empowering and heartbreaking. The photographer caught moments of me crying, lovingly touching my breasts, and saying goodbye. I wholeheartedly recommend this experience to any breast cancer patient. It's a beautiful way to honor and memorialize a part of yourself that you're about to lose.

After the boudoir shoot, I often took pictures of myself. It became a significant part of my healing journey, watching how my body healed itself after surgery and gradually returned to a new normal. I was in awe of my body's ability to knit itself back together after the surgeons had done their work. It made me wonder—what other body wisdom had I been completely oblivious to? My respect and relationship with my body changed forever.

Anyone who has suffered a loss like a mastectomy will understand how it can shatter your sense of womanhood. But I was so committed to being alive that I felt an intense need to be intimate with my lover shortly after my surgery—just six days after, to be exact. I had six drains hanging from my body, looking like grenades filled with disgusting fluid, and I was still in an epic amount of pain. But I pinned those drains to the back of my lingerie and had sex anyway. It was almost like I needed to feel alive again. I wouldn't recommend this to anyone, and my partner at the time was probably terrified of hurting me. But it was necessary for me, at that moment. In the aftermath, he would tease me about making him have sex with me while I was on "life support," and it would make me giggle.

After the surgery, I couldn't bring myself to continue with the Tantric breast massages. I was too squeamish to touch my scars, and the pain and numbness brought back a lot of trauma and fear. It took me a long time to feel comfortable with my new breasts. But I maintained a routine of self-pleasure almost daily, incorporating a Tantric jade egg practice. Looking back, I realize that I was using my sexual energy to heal. With so much pain—both emotional and physical—pleasuring myself gently and with respect was like giving myself healing medicine. Our sexual energy is powerful. It's the same energy that creates life. I used that energy to circulate through my body and heal during my cancer journey.

One of the most remarkable moments in my recovery happened during a surgery I had where I was awake. My surgeon was removing patches of skin over my nipples from the tissue transplant, which had, unbelievably, started to grow pubic hair because it came from my abdominal area. He injected freezing into my breasts, but as he worked, I could still feel everything. He was surprised because patients are usually told not to expect much sensation for at least a year, if ever. We were only six weeks post-op, and yet here I was, feeling everything. I told him about my meditative practice, about how I had talked to my abdominal tissue and told it that it was going to be my new breasts. He was astonished, saying he'd never seen anyone with this much sensitivity after surgery.

To my amazement, I still experience a lot of pleasure from my breasts. I can even orgasm as if I still have nipples. It's nothing short of miraculous, and I strut around like the miracle that I am. Some people get mad when they hear this. They have nipples and don't know how to orgasm with them; and here I am, nipple-less and still able to experience that pleasure. It's one of the reasons I've changed careers to become a sex coach. I want to help people connect with their bodies and treat them like beloved pets. Your body is your best friend. It's the only thing that's with you from your first breath to your last. Why on earth are we taught to hate our bodies? It's beyond me.

Cancer has changed me in so many ways, both for better and for worse. One of the most positive changes has been my introduction to dragon boating. This sport, which I started as part of my recovery, has been instrumental in reducing my risk of cancer recurrence and gaining psychosocial support from other breast cancer survivors. In three years, I've earned many gold medals. Dragon boating is gruelling, but it's incredibly beneficial for a survivor. One of the greatest benefits is being surrounded by other women who've been through what you've been through. When you're spat out of the medical system after surgery and treatment, you're left with a terrible hangover—trauma, emotional wounds, physical deficiencies, and the challenge of finding your place in the world again.

Competing with other survivors is inspiring. You can see people who are further along in their survivorship journey, and you can follow their pace. We train almost year-round—indoors in the gym and on ice during the winter and then on the water as soon as the ice melts. There's something profoundly healing about learning to paddle in sync with others. After cancer, it helps you sync back up to the pace of the world. It's a safe space to regain your strength. For the first few years, it's about rebuilding your body and feeling normal again. Later, it's about training for any future fights with cancer. I'm preparing myself to be "strong as f**k," so if cancer ever comes back, I'll be ready to win the fight a second time.

The journey through cancer has been one of the most intense, transformative experiences of my life. It's taught me the depth of my own resilience, the importance of self-love, and the incredible power of sexual energy as a healing force. I've learned to cherish my body as my closest companion, to treat it with the love and respect it deserves, and to use pleasure as a way to nourish and heal myself.

If I could teach anything to my younger self, it would be this: Pleasure is your birthright, a gift as natural as the breath in your lungs or the beat of your heart. It's not something you need to earn or justify. The world will tell you that pleasure is indulgence, that it's selfish or frivolous, but that couldn't be further from the truth. Pleasure is nourishment for the soul, a vital part of what makes us human. It connects us to our most authentic selves, grounding us in the present moment and reminding us of the beauty of life, even amidst its challenges.

As you move through life, you'll come to realize that your body is the nightclub of the soul. It's the place where your spirit dances, where joy and pain, love and loss all come together in a beautiful, chaotic rhythm. Your body isn't just a vessel carrying you from one day to the next—it's a living, breathing extension of who you are. Every experience and every emotion are etched into your muscles, bones, and skin. It's your history, your story, written in your flesh.

Make peace with your body early on because you don't just have a body—you *are* your body. This might sound like a subtle difference, but it's profound. We're often taught to think of our bodies as separate from ourselves, something to be controlled, improved, or even fought against. But the truth is, your body and soul are one. When you reject your body, you're rejecting a part of yourself. When you embrace your body, flaws and all, you're embracing the whole of who you are.

Imagine yourself as the computer, and your body as the droid. You've been paired together for life until death do you part. This partnership is the most intimate relationship you'll ever have, more enduring than any other. The sooner you start working together, the better. It's not just about making peace with your body, it's about forming a deep, loving relationship with it. Listen to it, learn from it, and honor it. Your body has its own wisdom, a kind of intelligence that's different from your mind but just as powerful. It knows when to rest, when to move, and when to heal. Trust it.

This journey is like a three-legged race where you, your body, and your spirit are bound together. You can only move as fast as the slowest one. If you're constantly at war with your body, or if you ignore your spirit, you'll find yourself stumbling and struggling to move forward. But when all three run together in harmony, you're as fast as lightning. You become a force of nature, unstoppable and free.

Working together doesn't mean everything will be easy. There will be times when your body falters because it feels like a burden rather than a blessing. There will be moments when your spirit feels heavy, weighed down by the trials of life. But these are the times when it's most important to be gentle with yourself and to remember that you're in this race together. When one part of you struggles, the others can help carry the load—your mind can offer encouragement, your spirit can provide hope, and your body can remind you of your strength.

In this race, it's not about who's the fastest or the most perfect. It's about moving forward, step by step, with grace and compassion. It's about understanding that the journey is as important as the destination and that every stumble is an opportunity to learn, grow, and become more fully yourself.

If I could go back in time and speak to my younger self, I would tell her to stop worrying so much about what her body looks like and start focusing on how it feels. I'd tell her to dance, move, and revel in the joy of being alive. I'd tell her to listen to the whispers of her body, to heed its needs and honor its desires. I'd tell her to make pleasure a priority, not just as an act of self-care, but as a way of life.

Pleasure isn't just about physical sensation—it's about emotional and spiritual fulfillment too. It's about finding joy in the little things, like the warmth of the sun on your skin, the sound of laughter, or the taste of your favorite food. It's about savoring each moment, even the difficult ones because they're all part of the rich tapestry of life.

Your body is the vehicle through which you experience all of this. It's your dance partner in the nightclub of the soul, and together, you create the rhythm of your life. When you're in sync, when you move together with love and respect, the dance becomes effortless, and life becomes a celebration.

So, to my younger self, and anyone reading this: Embrace your body. Love it fiercely. Cherish every moment you have with it. Make peace with it early on because it's not just your body—it's you. And when you run this race together, mind, body, and spirit, you'll discover that you're capable of more than you ever imagined. You'll find that you're as fast as lightning and that the journey, with all its ups and downs, is a beautiful, miraculous dance worth celebrating every step of the way.

Jessica Soodeen

Jessica Soodeen is no stranger to challenges and faces them head-on! Throughout her personal life and career, she has pushed boundaries and broken barriers. Whether on stage, at a racetrack, or in an office setting, Jessica has a unique ability to make everyone she encounters feel seen and heard. Her energy, filled with curiosity and wonder, is contagious.

As a child, Jessica lived overseas due to her father's work, gaining cultural insights at a young age. After returning to Calgary, Alberta, she built on this global perspective. Her first career as a mechanical design engineer took her around the world. However, her adventurous spirit led her to a new challenge: earning a master's degree in Motorsport Race Engineering. This pivot, born from her passion for road racing motorcycles—a hobby she picked up later in life—opened new avenues for her. Jessica has worked as a track-side engineer and driver coach, fully immersing herself in the world of motorsports. She even built her own motors in her living room, pulled wrenches for other teams, and immediately began coaching others on mindset.

Now, Jessica uses all these experiences to deliver dynamic keynote speeches that teach emotional and social intelligence lessons like no other.

Connect with Jessica:

[Jessica Soodeen | Linktree](#)

Chapter 7

The Art of Forgiveness at Full Throttle

By Jessica Soodeen

My heart and soul are on fire as I'm about to embark on my very first motorcycle race EVER! We are lined up in a grid, three motorcycles wide and three rows deep. There are two other motorcycle racers on either side of me. We are staggered slightly at the beginning of a long straight part of the racetrack. Thoughts of imposter syndrome creep in—"I've only been riding for five years," "I'm not ready to be in an actual race," and "I could get hurt if I get mixed up with faster riders"—but I must put them all aside because the "2 Minutes to Start" board has just been shown, and I don't have time for those thoughts. That board tells us racers that the green flag to GO will be waved in two minutes.

    I take a deep breath and remember that I am courageous, skilled, and about to put my training into ACTION! It's time to shift my brain to the task at hand! The motorcycle's V-twin engine is purring and it's time to twist the throttle for launch. To do this, you slightly turn your right hand counterclockwise, holding the handlebar similarly to how you would a screwdriver. My nerves get the better of me and my engine screams for a moment. I release the throttle and take a breath. Remembering my practice starts, I look down quickly at the dials on the bike to ensure my engine is roaring enough to accelerate but not too high. The other bikes around me are doing the same with anticipation of the green flag dropping to signal the start of the race. I only have my left toe touching the ground—which is about all I can manage being a rather short woman—while others may have the ball of their foot down or their foot flat on the ground. Show-offs! My right foot is on the footrest peg, and I am pushing down on the rear brake pedal to keep the motorcycle stopped.

My body is shaking, my hands are sweating inside my gloves, and the sun is beating down on my back. My eyes focus on the flag worker in the tower to the right who has the green flag up and ready to drop. My heart is pounding, and now my foot is barely on the ground with the anticipation. The flag drops and I let out the clutch; the bike bucks a bit and the race begins!

There's a long straightaway before the first turn and my focus is to shift through the gears smoothly. Unfortunately, I released the clutch lever too quickly and the engine bogged down. This mistake sends my bike forward sluggishly rather than launching like a rocket. I see the other racers zoom by as if they are running on dry ground while I'm wading through waist-deep water. This is crushing, but I don't have time to dwell on it. I must tell myself to stay focused on catching up, and not beat myself up. By the time we reach the first corner, I'm travelling at almost 200 km/hr, and there is no time to think about anything except hitting the brakes as the first turn approaches. But damn it, the thoughts come all the same: "Really, Jessica?! You bomb the start of your first-ever race? How are you going to catch up now?"

Despite this, I manage to stay focused on MY race—remembering the race line, where to turn, when to brake, when to roll back on the gas, and to push those limits with every lap. I am not bothered by the other two racers who pass me because my engineering brain had calculated the difference in lap times before the race even began. I was expecting this. However, when they pass me again on the second last turn, my negative thoughts come creeping back in. This means they have completed two full laps more than me for the duration of the race and have come in first and second place. Yet, I cross the finish line with pride because I've just completed my first race without crashing.

The experience taught me a lesson that I put into practice immediately. I realized I wouldn't have time to let it sink in, to journal about it, to meditate on it, or anything else that takes time. The next race was only one short hour away. I didn't have time to beat myself up or to ruminate in regret. The lesson was to quickly forgive myself and extract the learnings equally fast. This lesson of self-forgiveness would prove to be paramount in my racing for the next five years of competition and would be instrumental in my life.

Another effective analogy exists on the tennis court, for those not into motorsports. Tennis players who make mistakes on a shot will face the same ball coming right back at them within seconds, so they also have no time to beat themselves up. They must be ready for that ball and play at their best right away!

If you think that motorcycle road racing (as opposed to dirt bike riding) is a bit of a crazy hobby, you are right! Unlike many of my competitors, I did not grow up in this sport. I was in my second last year of university completing a bachelor's degree in mechanical engineering when I "won" motorcycle lessons at a fundraiser. The event supported a local mechanical engineering club, the Formula SAE team, that designs and builds an open-wheel race car (meaning there isn't a body covering the wheels similar to Formula 1), and then races it against other universities. I was NOT on their team. I'd never ridden a motorcycle, nor did I ever watch Formula 1 races or any other type of motorsports. But I had friends on the team and wanted to support their event. The irony would not be lost on me, that they figured I had a bit of a wild side, and that motorcycle riding would light me up! Hence, the reason why I put won in quotes; winning that prize was a little rigged.

I rode on the street for four years before doing that first race. Each summer, I went to the local racetrack, Race City Speedway, in Calgary to hone my skills. Riding motorcycles on the street comes with big risks—left-turn bandits, poles, leaves on the ground, cars, trucks, gravel… you get the idea. Track days and nights provided a safe place to learn to ride on debris-free asphalt, with everyone going in the same direction, an ambulance on site, and everyone wearing head-to-toe safety gear. It's also a great place to get faster in a controlled environment, which I thought I was doing, only to be lapped twice in my first race.

It was in that fourth year at one of those track days that someone commented to me about my riding: "You're not very fast, but you are very comfortable in traffic. You know, you could race and probably get faster and more safely than those hooligans who are new and riding the wheels off their bikes." I didn't need to hear anything more. The next day, I was in my garage figuring out how to take the headlights, signal lights, kickstand, and a whole bunch of "street parts" off my bike. I also promised myself that I would sign up for race school the following spring. There it was. I began road racing motorcycles with not even a handful of years of riding experience. Little did I know where it was going to take me!

Around the same time, I started a full-time job, as opposed to being a contract mechanical design engineer. Stability was important as I'd bought the other half of the duplex I owned and lived in, and this new hobby was not cheap. It was a joke around the racetracks that some of us were sponsored by Visa and MasterCard, although none of us had any decals to complete the gag. The more I got involved in racing—on my own and with other teams—the more I realized this hobby was turning into a passion. I considered combining it with my career by looking into master's and doctoral degree programs in motorsport engineering of some sort overseas! This passion escalated to a quasi-obsession when I decided that, to lead mechanics, I should know a bit about that job. I certainly was not interested in obtaining a full-on technician certification, especially since I was already working full-time.

I decided to do the next best thing by importing a motorcycle from New Zealand that required regular engine maintenance throughout the race season. It was physically smaller than the one I started with but was nimbler and faster around the corners. It was a "real" race bike. I even requested and received a letter from Yamaha's Japanese headquarters stating it was a competition-only vehicle to facilitate the importation. This little machine, named Bunny, would serve as a tool to prepare me for my dream of combining my newfound passion with my engineering background.

Once shipped from Vancouver's port to a warehouse in Calgary, I had the delivery truck bring it to my front door and right into my living room! This marked the beginning of assembling three motors every winter for the next couple of years. The credibility this gave me was invaluable, as engineers often receive criticism for not being hands-on enough. The motorcycle came with a ton of spare parts, as well as the parts with which to build motors, plus a Japanese manual! The internet at the time was not what it is now. So, I had an English manual sent to me by snail mail from a fellow racer I met at a forum.

Fast forward a few years, I have successfully assembled my own motors, secured sponsors, and written a few articles in motorcycle magazines and newspapers nationwide. I was also accepted into a master's program in the Basque Country in northern Spain, where I earned the degree and began a career as a freelance race car engineer and professional formula driving coach. I have worked in various feeder classes to F1, which is where you can have a broader career within the sector.

Throughout my career, the lesson of self-forgiveness is one that I've passed on to the drivers I've coached and something I continue to practice myself. A big part of forgiving yourself quickly is knowing that you have done your best to prepare. By doing so, you will likely gain NEW insights from mistakes and/or oversights.

But what does "prepare" look like in the world of motorsports?

Preparation involves one of my favorite aspects of the job: track walks and subsequent visualization exercises. This starts almost as soon as the drivers arrive at the track. We would print out maps of the tracks, sometimes bring a couple of tablets that had some fast lap videos loaded on them and go for a stroll. These afternoon strolls were a deliberate and strategic exercise. We went from corner to corner, looking at new bumps in the track, any new pavement patches or transitions where there would be less grip and updated signage. It is best to notice these things at a walking pace. We would discuss which references to use for when to hit the brakes, when to turn in the car, and when to hit the gas and accelerate out of the corners. Since drivers sit so low in these cars, we would hunch down and look around at the same height as sitting in the car to simulate the perspective.

Now, I was fortunate to work with a team competing in the World Series by Renault! This took me to some of the best tracks in Europe, period! It was delightful to get such a close-up look at these iconic places where motorsports history was made! Not that I would be able to speak on that with my colleagues yet, since I had no background on this. I would explain how, up until that point, I was a doer in the field, not a watcher. But I digress; the point is that I was at world-class facilities whose track lengths could vary between 3.5 to 7 kilometres. Quite the afternoon meander!

Once back in the paddock, we reviewed the driver's notes, watched more videos, and used cheat sheets the team provided. It was time to dive into visualization exercises. Similar to when I am on stage delivering a keynote address to a professional association and taking the audience on an emotional visualization exercise, I guide the drivers through a mental visualization of a lap on the racetrack. Sometimes we would even time it! I taught the drivers the value of being prepared at a new level. These tracks are more complex than the go-kart tracks they were used to as they progressed through car classes.

I had them visualize things going sideways, which would bring me right back to that crappy start on my very first motorcycle race. How could I help them work on building the neuropaths of resilience? What were the explicit techniques for this? Some younger drivers felt quite silly when I had them get into their parked race car and go through a lap of the track in their heads. This was not an uncommon practice; however, I did it a little differently. Once they had mentally done a lap or two, I'd ask them to tell me where they were on the track. I would throw a curve ball and tell them that they made a mistake and ask them to talk through the recovery.

In racing, you are going so fast out on the track that if you mess up a corner, another one is coming right up! It's just like that tennis ball analogy I shared before. I would coach them that on the track, they don't have time to beat themselves up. They only have time to remember what reference point they messed up and nail it the next lap, and the lap after that, until the race or qualification is done.

When these flubs happen and the sessions are over, I permit them to get angry, feel disappointed, swear, pray, run, feel dismayed, or express sadness—whatever they need. But once the emotions are truly felt and processed, it is time to pluck out the lessons.

In a way, we are all like race drivers. We navigate this track called life, with all its twists and turns. We race through some stretches, yet there are some corners where we proceed with caution. We make mistakes but we keep moving forward toward the finish line because what matters at the end are the lessons we learned along the way.

So, I ask you…

How long does it take YOU to move on from a mistake?

How do you know when you need to pivot out of that headspace?

When is it appropriate to dissect a blunder and when to just let go?

Who do you want to be when it comes to reframing your missteps?

Jessica Lee

Jessica Lee is the owner and operator of Always Sparkling Cleaning Company. She was born and raised in Ontario, Canada. She moved to Calgary in 2019 since she has longed for the mountains after living briefly in Banff in her early twenties. Her brilliant passion for helping others extends from a wide background of cleaning services, including hospitality in the tourism industry and as an environmental service worker.

As a single mother and strong female leader, Jessica has dedicated her time to serving others around her community, including leading a fundraiser for the Women in Need Society (WINS). When she moved to Calgary, she used her passion for cleaning and service to inspire her successful cleaning business. In her chapter, Jessica provides insight into the difficulties of familial expectations which she draws upon her personal obstacles. These have led her to embody a perspective of self-acceptance and perseverance, striving to illuminate the power of expectations and relationships.

Connect with Jessica:
https://alwayssparkling.ca/

Chapter 8

Dare to Dream

By Jessica Lee

For as long as I can remember, I've always dreamed of leaving the small town where I was raised and making a difference in the world. My parents would call me a dreamer with her head in the clouds. Yet, they always supported even my poorest decisions while I found my footing on who I wanted to become.

At 19, I packed my little blue Chevy Malibu as full as possible, with everything from my clothes to my stereo, and set out on the adventure that would later shape much of my life. It felt like my own "Wide Open Spaces" moment that I always longed for. I headed from my small hometown in Ontario to the magnificent Rocky Mountains in Banff, Alberta. I instantly knew, the moment I entered Banff for the first time and got my first look at Cascade Mountain, that this adventure would change my life! I had never truly experienced a breathtaking moment before this one, and boy, was it incredible!

For the next six years, I bounced around various parts of Canada, trying to find my place in the world. When you are born a dreamer, you're always looking for your next great adventure to fulfill the fire in your soul and passion in your heart. That was what I was longing for, and I knew that I was never going to find it in a small Ontario town with a cow statue at its core. While bouncing around Canada, I had the privilege to explore the beautiful Canadian desert of Osoyoos, which would also be the place where I lost one of the biggest influences in my life, my papa. I have also lived five minutes from the beach in the beautiful, small wine-country city of Penticton, where I happily walked from one end of town to the other almost every day. Walking the beach length nightly with music blasting in my headphones was easily one of my fondest memories of that period in my life. I eventually headed back to my roots in Ontario and explored several other cities along the way, including London, Brampton, and Peterborough.

I became more resilient with every new challenge life handed me, as each one also added a new level of strength that I didn't know was possible. I often navigated each challenge alone, or with very little support. With every obstacle I faced, my parents asking when I would settle down and stay put somewhere echoed in the back of my mind. I could envision them rolling their eyes at my next "great idea" and how little money was in the bank every time I was ready to make my next move. I was still shaping the person I was yet to become and building the resilient woman I can confidently call myself today. Not even they could stop me from stepping outside of the safe comfort of normalcy to experience all that life had to offer.

The goal of being a nurse had been on the horizon for as long as I can remember. Everyone tells you to find a good career, with good pay, and I loved working with people and helping others. I headed off to college and later bridged to a Bachelor of Science in Nursing program, only to end up dropping out when my mental health was eating me at my core. I knew I needed to make a change, but I didn't know why. So I filed a withdrawal and headed home to figure out what was next. So many people told me I'd never return to school. Comments like, "You need to do something more with your life," left me feeling lost, alone, and with no sense of direction or purpose for what I thought my family expected me to be. "Be a nurse. They make good money. You can help people. Smart people get nursing jobs." While intended with love, these comments drove me into the most depressive moments of my life. My inner voice would whisper, "I guess I'm just not good enough to be what they want me to be." I also thought this was what I wanted, but the longing for adventure was stronger.

We often get so complacent in life to just accept the next steps because "it is what it is." We simply don't believe in ourselves and often, there isn't anyone other than our inner voice whispering that we fight for more. But I have never let that voice in my head be silenced. You see, I was a daydreamer—someone who would run outside and dance in the rain like I was still a young girl. I've always aimed to live for more than the day-to-day tasks and adult normalcy. However, I am part of a family that thrives on normalcy, structure, and expected outcomes. I was a step outside the box they had built, with a longing to find my calling and create the life I had always dreamed about. I could not let that box stop me from finding my intended path.

Along the journey to discovering the version of me that longed to live outside the box, I navigated many big challenges that could have broken me. But instead, these urged me to grow up quickly and never pass up on an opportunity, no matter how big or small. This is what I hope to remind you to do too! From losing every dollar that I had to a commission-based, unethical job, to being diagnosed with cancer and eventually given six months to live, and everything in between, it certainly has not been an easy feat. We so often get caught up in the day-to-day and forget how to live in the moment of spontaneity. Tomorrow is never promised and the version of you today can always choose a new path if that's what your soul longs for.

Embrace the version of yourself you strive to become, in the shadow of what society has told you to be. Without that spark fighting to shine through and by not following your heart's burning desires, you forget who you are and what you were put on this incredible planet to accomplish. You won't know how amazing your life can be until you leap outside of your comfort zone to follow the dreams you've always longed for. Take the trip, change your career, or uproot your life to find the place that's meant to be called home. Have the hard conversations. Whatever the case may be, never be afraid to follow that inner voice that's longing for something new. These changes can be scary—heck, I still get scared every time a new one arises. But then I step back and think of my last hard decision and how that outcome changed my life. I remind myself that I can do the hard things, and they are worth every difficult hurdle that gets input into my journey.

We can either grow old and tell our grandchildren about the amazing leaps and bounds we took to build the life we love, or we can tell them about our regrets, missed opportunities, and how we want more for them. I refuse to allow that to be any of our stories. We deserve the life we long for our children and grandchildren just as much as they do!

I got complacent for a while by working eight-hour shifts, day in and day out, cleaning the hospital ICU. It was rewarding and fulfilling, and as close as I felt I could get to the nursing career I longed for but didn't think was the right next step. The management of the company I worked for was terrible. They would overwork and scold you every time you didn't complete your entire task list on a busy night. Their reward for hard work was a pizza party every six months. This became my normal, with a daily expected outcome, until one day it didn't. I decided that I was done living in the complacency of a "good wage with benefits and a pension plan," and chose to take my life back.

What We Know Now

I woke up one morning and knew it was time for a change, and that there was no better time for a big leap than now! I searched the internet to find a place to rent that was neither in the town I was currently in nor my hometown. I pondered a few new places, weighing the pros and cons for each, and my heart landed on Calgary. It's a short drive to those beautiful mountains I've longed to be back in since I was 20. While it didn't have the same hustle and bustle of a big city like Toronto, it had enough of the city lifestyle to be excited for. The best of both worlds! Finding a rental was easier than expected, and it was time to break the news to my parents. I knew if I had told them about my idea before finding a place, they would try to talk me out of it (and frankly, they might have succeeded). I felt so defeated and lacked confidence that their arguments could have won over my mind easily. My parents were unsure what I was thinking and how long this new adventure would last. Despite this, they asked me, in worried tones, what I needed from them to make it happen and what was next.

A few weeks later, with a trailer loaded to the brim after an epic game of Tetris, and with my dog and cat in tow, my mom loaded up her truck and off we went on a road trip across Canada to get me to my newfound home. My mom has never told me outright, but I know it always breaks her heart to give me away to a new city and leave a piece of her heart there while she heads home to live out her own goals and dreams. I packed up my entire life with about $2,000 in the bank, no job, and a longing for something new. I was officially settled in a new city where I didn't know anybody and was 3,000 km from the place that had always been home. I was in for an adventure, one that could've broken many, but my drive to succeed kept me trudging even in the muddiest of waters.

A few weeks had gone by with no luck finding a steady job. I was just picking up random babysitting gigs where I could, to make sure I could pay rent and put food on the table. Two months went by, and other than being a self-employed contractor cleaning houses, I still had no real job. So I decided to take things into my own hands and started advertising myself on Facebook Marketplace and Kijiji. Before I knew it, I had gathered a handful of clients and between cleaning and babysitting, I had a full-time gig. There I was, waking up and getting on the city bus at 6:30 every morning, dragging my supplies along with me, then getting home long enough to swap my cleaning supplies for some dinner and babysitting games before heading out to care for some kiddos.

Within about eight weeks, I had enough of a steady schedule of cleaning jobs that I was able to minimize babysitting to periodic gigs and focus on cleaning. We were on a roll. I was excited and loved what I was doing! Four months into this newfound passion and career, however, the world shut down because of COVID-19, leaving everything I had just worked so hard to build in complete uncertainty. I had no choice but to stop services, hang out at home, and hope for the best. I was immunocompromised at the time, still not a full year out of my last chemotherapy and terrified to leave my home.

A few weeks later, I found out I was about to be on an even crazier adventure. I was six weeks pregnant and preparing for my greatest adventure of all—motherhood! I pondered what I would do next. "How am I going to clean while pregnant?" "Will my clients come back when this pandemic is over?" I could have let these thoughts destroy me right then and there, and begin on an entirely new path, but I was happy doing what I loved. There was nobody to tell me when I could or could not take time off. I was living the entrepreneurial dream.

Summer came, and cleaning was finally acknowledged as an essential service. This was the time when the uncertainty would all play out—were we going to thrive, or did we have to shut our doors? To my surprise, when we reached out to our incredible client base, they were **ALL** ready and excited to have us back. Many of them also shared our name with their colleagues, family, and friends. We had an absolutely full schedule and no room for more. But we still had to break the news to my client base that I was expecting and figure out how we would navigate that next! Of course, it wasn't hard to break the news as my belly was very large and in charge by the time I was back in their homes! I pondered what would happen next. Should I take a few weeks of leave and hope our clients will wait for us again? Should I hire some subcontractors to fulfill the work in the interim? Could I just go clean with a baby in a carrier?

After much contemplation, I decided it was time to hire and train a subcontractor to take on my role so I could take a few months off to care for my new baby. Just a mere seven days before delivering my daughter, you could still find me attempting to clean bathtubs, propping my belly onto the tub so I could reach. Many gasped in awe when they heard this, but I was only doing what needed to be done to keep my dream alive and provide for my incoming daughter.

Little did I know, my sweet little Friday the 13th baby was coming into this world hell on wheels, with a fight like no other. Diagnosed with a rare genetic condition, she turned blue in my room at eight hours old and spent some time in the NICU and Care floor at the children's hospital. I knew those amazingly thought-out plans I had created were once again going to need to pivot to provide for my daughter. After 18 months, two surgeries, two ICU stays, a feeding tube, and a dozen specialists later, we made it through, while continuing to grow my business and navigate life along the way. It was a time that could have broken me and would have broken many. But we got through it simply because I fought so hard to keep my dream alive and continued to push through the unknown to create the life I longed for.

Four and a half years later, that cleaning company I started from a Kijiji ad on a city bus, now employs six people, feeds their families and mine, provides peace of mind and takes away the overwhelm of many families in our own communities! Had I let any of these hiccups take my spark, my fire would have gone out, and I certainly would have failed. But I didn't let the tough life challenges, the words of others around me, or anything else dull that fire within me. Instead, I made lemonade out of the lemons. I acknowledged that no matter where life takes me, there will always be difficult scenarios to overcome. It is what we find within us that will push us to succeed, sometimes even beyond anything we could ever imagine accomplishing.

All of this is to say that every person has a dream. Some of us shove them deep into our beings and avoid them because we believe they simply aren't achievable, while others use them as the wood that continues to keep the fire inside burning to accomplish them. We all have burdens, obstacles, and challenges to overcome. You can overcome yours, too, when you find the courage to ignite the spark inside of you.

Linh Tran

Linh Tran, of Calgary, Alberta, has been a dedicated financial broker with World Financial Group for over 15 years. She has received senior levels within her business and consistently gets recognized as an MVP within her team.

Helping people reach their financial goals and protect their families is more than just a job for Linh… it's a passion. As someone who came from a refugee background, she's witnessed firsthand the incredible transformations that hard work and commitment can bring when paired with a good heart and the right intentions.

Through a financial services platform, she's been able to grow and develop herself into a business leader. The most exciting and rewarding part of her journey is who she's becoming and making a difference to those she has served and continues to help.

Connect with Linh:

[Linh C Tran | Linktree](#)

Chapter 9

If Only We Had More Money

By Linh Tran

Would you ever make a decision that might result in a more than 50 percent chance of your family perishing at sea? I'm not sure I could ever do that.

Well, that's what my parents had to do to get us out of Vietnam. My dad fought for South Vietnam during the war and knew that there was no future for his family there. Even though we were physically alive, mentally, emotionally, and spiritually, we were dead. I thank my parents every single day for making the courageous decision to flee Vietnam in the middle of the night on a fishing boat that my dad worked on. It was a fishing boat that typically held five fishermen, but there were 46 men, women and children literally squished in there, like sardines. Fortunately, we made it out… all of us, including my parents with three young children and five of my mom's siblings. We were at sea for three days without food or water, though we had lots of hope, prayer, and faith that we would be saved. Luckily, our prayers were answered. We were saved by a Dutch tanker in the South China Sea and brought to a refugee camp in Malaysia.

We stayed in the camp for eight months before going to Canada in October 1980. So, you can imagine growing up in Canada wasn't the same for me as with a typical Canadian. Coming to Canada at three years old, I watched my parents struggle to establish a new life for our family. Everything was so different. They needed to learn a new language, culture, and way of living, including adapting to a new weather system.

It was extremely challenging, and on top of it all, my dad had PTSD due to his involvement in the war. The only way he knew how to deal with it was with alcohol. He became an alcoholic for most of his life. Like most males, he didn't want to discuss his emotions and feelings. I didn't understand my dad's mental health issues or my parents' relationship dynamics. I'm not even certain my parents married for love.

My dad's alcoholism caused him to be very abusive to my mom. He would hurt my mom and take everything out on her. He never hurt his children. But what do you think it does to a child, witnessing the two people they love the most, one being abused by the other, and feeling helpless? I felt afraid for my mom and powerless.

My biggest fear as a child was becoming orphaned. I was afraid my dad would kill my mom and end up in prison. I wouldn't wish that upon anybody. Every time I asked, "Mom, why can't we leave Dad? Why do you have to deal with this abuse?" She gave me an answer I never accepted as my truth, but it was hers. She always said, "We are new to this country. I don't work outside the home. I don't speak the language. We don't have a big support network. I don't have resources. How am I supposed to take care of three young children on my own? Where am I going to go?" In my young mind, I took that to mean that if we had more money, my mom wouldn't need to put up with the beating, and I wouldn't have to be terrified of growing up an orphan. How many people still ask themselves these questions today? If only we had more money!

After high school, I took a gap year to enjoy myself and have some freedom. This made me realize that I needed to get away from my parents. The fighting still didn't stop, and neither did my dad's drinking. The abuse turned into arguments when my mom started menopause. Her rage, resentment, and anger finally came out. Sometimes, I actually felt bad as it seemed she instigated the fights. Menopause brought out the fighter in her. I guess that was payback for my dad's behavior.

I needed to find who I was because I was lost in all the expectations from my family as the go-to person for everything since the age of seven. I have 7-year-old nieces and nephews now who can barely get dressed or eat without making a mess. Yet, when I was at that age, it was cast upon me to start translating for my family—from government documents to visits to the doctor or dentist—you name it. Not to mention the numerous dealings with the police when my mom called them in on my dad. I translated because I didn't know any different. I just wanted my parents to approve of me. I wanted them to be happy with me. I didn't want to get in trouble because I wanted my parents' approval. Being addicted to the approval of those in your life is a real thing. Approval addiction is such a strong urge that you will do whatever it takes to get approval from the people you love, respect, and admire even though they're the ones who may cause you pain.

I had a great relationship with my dad, especially later in life, but that didn't take away the biggest fear I had growing up. As our life in Canada continued, I grew tired of watching my parents fight. I slowly grew tired of caring so much and dealing with the chaos and noise. I often thought I could fix my parents' relationship if I was a good girl and did well in school. If I did everything they asked and pleased them, would that make them happy and not fight anymore? How silly I was to think that as a little girl. As an adult, I realized that the approval addiction so many people have in life stems from their childhood. Wanting attention and care from the people they love the most plants an unconscious seed to need approval from everyone.

I finally gave myself grace not to feel like it was my responsibility to fix my parents' issues, no matter how much I cared for their well-being. It was their deal and only they could fix it for themselves. The best way I figured to get away from all the chaos was to go where no one could call me. I went to work on cruise ships for nine years. The beautiful part was that I got to go with my partner, and we sailed wherever the ship went. We worked in the casino department where most of the action was, had a lot of fun, and met many great people.

My parents didn't want me to work that far away from home, but they knew they couldn't stop me. The only reason that helped put them at ease with my decision was that they didn't have to explain to anyone in the family that I was with a same-gender partner. Yes, I'll leave that story for another chapter.

The nine years working on ships with my partner gave me the space and time to discover who I was and who I wanted to be. I started to find out more about what I valued and stood for. In my thirties, I decided I wanted to be in business. I didn't know what kind of business I wanted to do, but I always envisioned myself being a successful businesswoman. Maybe it was the movies I watched growing up, and seeing the authority, control, and power in rich businesspeople.

After working on cruise ships from age 21 to 29, I was done with that phase of my life. My partner and I settled back in Calgary since that's where all our family were, and I did a couple of odd jobs. One was in management, as an assistant spa director for my sister's company. She built a beautiful spa, but unfortunately, it closed after a year due to the global financial crisis in 2008. What I realized then was that if you're working for someone else, you may not have a job the next day, no matter who you are working for. That experience helped me decide whatever I did next, I wanted to be certain I would have a job every single day for the rest of my life. Earning what I was truly worth and having a positive impact was also at the top of my checklist.

While job seeking, someone reached out and shared with me an opportunity in the financial services industry. I didn't know this company existed at that time, but when I saw that it could give me the chance to earn whatever I wanted, work for myself and do something meaningful… I was in. It checked off all my boxes and has given me so much more that I didn't know was possible. Control of my time is the biggest privilege of all.

I find it interesting that the two longest careers I've had both involved dealing with money. Of course, in different ways. The casino trained me to take people's money for a living, that's the nature of what a casino dealer does. Now, I aim to help people find money and put it back in their pockets. I look at it as a little bit of penance, as I was very proficient at taking people's money in my casino days. It was too bad I didn't get paid a commission for that. I would've been retired at 30.

It's so rewarding because of who I have become in this business. Not only do I help families and people who are overlooked by the traditional financial services industry, but I also get to build more business leaders alongside me. After 15 years in this business, it's still fun. I've grown so much more confident and my belief in myself increases continually. I'm so blessed for the mentors and coaches I have met in the business and still get to work with every day. Regardless of all the challenges in building a business and developing a team, it is worth it. I have learned so many things I never expected to, like not being ashamed of my upbringing and that it's OK to be vulnerable.

I worked through the story of my past while attending a Make Your Mark program with Colin Sprake. I cried a lot on the day that I got to share my story. The crying was me grieving the death of the old me. The shedding of my tears was like the shedding of my shame. That's when it hit me—the reason why I do what I do today, and I started sharing my story in small doses. The feedback and response I received was not what I expected. It was positive and moving. People resonated with it and wanted to hear more. They thanked me for being brave and having the courage to speak of it. I had never seen myself in the light of those words before and I started to shift. My self-image, self-doubt, self-esteem, and self-love all shifted. I began to build a new identity.

I never felt I was a victim in any of this. I never had a "poor me" attitude. I just felt helpless because I couldn't protect my mom and I couldn't fix my dad's problems. I wanted to save their marriage. I believe they should have split up, but they didn't. They had all four children in agreement to separate, but they didn't. Their refusal to separate taught me another thing... whatever you believe in, you don't give up on. They believed in the sacredness of marriage, and they were together until my dad passed away in 2014. Their decision taught me the value of committing to and fighting for what you believe in, even if it wasn't easy because the right thing isn't always easy to do. Right and wrong is a perspective based on our values and morals. I undoubtedly know my parents taught me great morals and values. More importantly, they wanted me to become better at who I am and who I am becoming.

I stopped being ashamed of my story and what I went through. More than that, I stopped being ashamed of growing up poor and growing up being bullied. All that has helped build my resilience and mental toughness. These are qualities that I needed to have to be in business for this long.

What is it that we can believe in ourselves? I've always believed that I can learn and improve, that I'm a good person, and that I want to do good for others. When I felt helpless watching my parents fight as I was growing up, I knew that I never wanted to feel like that ever again. I never wanted to be in a position where I couldn't be helpful or didn't have a solution. It is clear now that other people's problems are not mine to resolve. I will be there to support them and offer insight, if needed, but I cannot fix it for them. Doing it all for other people does not empower them to be capable and independent. Self-belief and confidence are what many people need more of. They gain that by being self-reliant.

Although my parents were not a fitting example of what a healthy relationship and partnership looked like, they still thought they were entitled not to allow me to be with a same-gender partner when I came out to them. Yes, they actually said, "You are not allowed to be gay! Go to the doctor, you are sick." The funny thing is that my doctor at the time was also gay. I wonder what kind of medication he would've given me. Seriously, I can't even make this up.

My resilience helped me break through the lack of approval of my parents, siblings and the people close in my life. That realization freed me to be true to myself and do what I believed was right. It is my responsibility to make myself happy, and nobody else's. Just like I am not responsible for anyone else's happiness. Being a good person is what I knew growing up and that should count for something.

I knew that my parent's beliefs about certain things were not mine and that I should seek my own truth. My business has allowed me to do just that, and to find my purpose by serving people and helping them with their money; especially with knowing what money has meant to me over the years. It is a resource that helps eliminate anxiety, worries, and fears that so many people have in life. It is a source of energy to be shared and used to support others. Many of the decisions we make are directly related to the amount of money we have or don't have. The clothes we wear, the car we drive, the house we live in, the school our children go to, the vacations we take, and even the food we eat are based on how much we can afford. Money ranks right up there with oxygen…we need it to live!

My story has shaped me into who I am today—a leader in the financial services industry, a caring businesswoman who makes her own decisions on who I help and how I help them. I am blessed to have my own business where I can serve the less fortunate. Wealth isn't just about money. Wealth comes in many forms. I am rich in health and relationships. I have lots of love in my life. I have great friends. I have family members who respect me and appreciate me because I've endured. They didn't all support my business journey in the beginning as they do now because the results are starting to show.

I am thankful for the experiences I had as they have led me to a business I love. I can help people learn about resources and provide a network they can rely on for support to get out of their unfortunate situation. For most people, the reason why they don't leave abusive situations, even in the corporate world, I think, is because they don't believe there's a better place to understand and support them. I want to show them there's hope. Be good and do good just because you can.

Lisa Sobry

Lisa M. Sobry is a certified life coach, wellness healer, Reiki master and instructor, and psychic tarot card reader in Calgary, Alberta. She is also a trauma survivor and the author of nine published books, including this book compilation.

Through coaching sessions, healing practices, and writing, Lisa empowers women to break free from societal norms and limitations. Her work encourages women to embrace their personal power, pursue their dreams, and stand up for their beliefs. Join Lisa on a journey of spiritual growth, peace, happiness, and inner transformation.

Connect with Lisa:

https://linktr.ee/lisasobry

Chapter 10

Finding My Personal Power

By Lisa M. Sobry

As I gazed in the mirror observing the beautiful woman looking back at me, I saw a fire in her eyes I had never seen before. Sparkling brown eyes, soft tanned skin, brown hair with blonde highlights, and crazy natural curls reflected an image of a woman I had seen glimpses of over the years. Yet, this woman's reflection felt different. I noticed the soft lines around her eyes and forehead, but I did not focus on them, dwell on them, or criticize them as I would have before. Her slightly muscular toned body reflected her commitment and dedication to fitness and eating healthy. The stretch marks across her breasts and belly were the result of bearing three beautiful children. In the past, I had disliked them. I felt they ruined my perfect image of what a woman should look like. Now, I admire them. The woman staring back at me was a strong, powerful woman. She had survived trauma and unhealthy and abusive relationships. And here she stood, beautiful, kind, and authentic.

Our society teaches us that women should be soft and gentle and should dote on their male counterparts regardless of whether they are kind or abusive, bear children, complete all the household chores, cook meals, and work full-time jobs outside of the home. Somewhere, amid all the running around and providing for others, women lose who they truly are. They become stressed and fatigued, disregarding self-care because they do not have time in their busy schedules, forgetting that they are important. They are lost in day-to-day activities, feeling anxious about merely existing in a world they created and no longer understand. Thoughts of going to the gym, working out, doing yoga, or going for a walk quickly fade as the body shuts down after a busy day. Exhausted, they crawl into bed thinking of all the tasks they didn't complete and how they will be added to tomorrow's list.

Although great strides have been made in women's rights, we still do not seem to stand in our personal power. We struggle to identify who we are and where we belong in a society that is still dominated by men. How can we empower the next generation of young women? We can do so by leading by example. There is absolutely nothing wrong with a woman standing in her power. She voices her concerns healthily and is proud of who she is and what she brings to the world, whether it is being a stay-at-home mother, an entrepreneur, or the CEO of a corporation.

I used to be the "people pleasing" stay-at-home mother raising her children, the single mother attending school and then working. I have owned businesses and worked for corporations. Over the years, I've had two nervous breakdowns and was diagnosed by doctors and psychiatrists with mental illness. I was on antidepressants and anti-anxiety medication for years, keeping the symptoms at bay but never truly healing myself. Medication is merely a Band-Aid solution. It suppresses emotions, but the trauma is never dealt with. The same can be said about drugs and alcohol. It continues to cover the trauma, and the person never truly heals. I did not know what self-care was. I was too busy looking after everyone else and accomplishing the daily list of tasks I needed to complete. My childhood trauma was buried deep inside me and never talked about. However, it had an impact on who I was and the decisions I made in my life. I attracted abusive men with addictions, who lied to me about the life they would provide for me and my children. Once the truth was revealed, I packed up the children and moved, repeatedly. The aftermath of my parenting left my children vulnerable and made it difficult for them to manage their own stress and anxiety. The bonus of my parenting was raising two independent daughters and a son who respects and appreciates women.

It was a long journey for me. I did not know what personal power was or even that I had any. I spent most of my life in fight-or-flight mode—a well-known stress response that occurs when hormones are released in your body, prompting you to stay and fight or run and flee danger. My first abusive experience with a man occurred when I was three years old, and I have been running ever since. If I stood my ground, a hand or a fist would come towards me in anger. In 2018, I found a counsellor who provided me with the tools I needed for my healing journey towards empowerment. She taught me what self-care was all about, how to quit fleeing, and that it was okay for me to say no.

Self-care means taking the time to do things that help you live well and improve your physical, mental, emotional, and spiritual health. It can also help you manage your stress levels. We do not have to live and be our emotions, but we do have to view and acknowledge them, and then let them go. As women, we are taught to be emotional and nurturing. Sadly, this is a societal role that is handed down from generation to generation. When we do finally heal, most of us have already passed the traits on to our daughters. I learned how to view decisions based on pros and cons and remove the emotional aspect. An example would be quitting a job and starting a new one. What are the financial aspects? Do I need to move? Are there housing or travel costs? What education level is required? Am I qualified for the position? There is no emotional aspect to this decision. Thinking about leaving behind the people I work well with would be adding emotions.

I started with Reiki classes and connected to my spiritual side. Reiki is a Japanese technique for stress reduction and relaxation that also promotes mental and physical healing. I loved it so much that I attended multiple levels and began to teach it. The meditations grounded me and pulled the racing thoughts from my mind. Next, I scheduled a pedicure every six weeks. I worked hard for my money and deserved to treat myself. It also relaxed my mind and made me feel more feminine. Then, I started seeing a hairstylist every two months, trying on different colors and hairstyles. They made me feel younger, refreshed and more vibrant. I went back to the gym and ate healthily. I walked into the gym on March 4, 2024, ready to "get back into shape" after a knee injury in 2023, and I left empowered, strong in my core and in who I was. Something shifted that day. I realized how much working out meant to me and that it was a key to my personal power. The "a-ha" moment I had waited for my entire life finally arrived!

When you are living true to what you believe and what is important to you, you are standing in your personal power. It means you acknowledge all you are capable of and know, and accept who you are—the good, the bad, and the not-so-pretty. You are authentic and you speak the truth. To be authentic means behaving in congruence with one's values, beliefs, motives, and personality dispositions. I am sure you have heard the saying, "Walk the talk." If you say you eat healthy, then you eat healthy. Standing in our power can be very liberating, allowing us to be true to ourselves and discover our worth. With power comes responsibility. It is easy to misuse our power by blaming, judging, or being critical of others. We need to always maintain a balance of power.

I've stood in my power before, on stage, speaking to eighty women about taking back their power and how they give it away. But this shift was different. I noticed I was more direct in my conversations and less about "telling the story." As I stood more in my personal power, friendships shifted. Old friends, whose lives were full of drama, left. New friendships were created with people who were empowered. I coined the phrase, "no drama mama," and used it whenever someone started telling their story. Some people said I was rude for cutting them off and I would explain, "It's your drama, not mine. I do not want to hear about it. How are you going to resolve the situation? The only person who can change your life is you!" I started reviewing the areas in my life where I had drama and made changes to quash it. The more confident I felt, the stronger my personal power became.

Setting boundaries with friends, family and yourself, and then keeping those boundaries help you stay in your power. It isn't selfish to say, "No, I don't want to eat that or go there." Eating healthy and living a clean addiction-free lifestyle (without obsessing) allows your body to feel strong. Engaging in spiritual activities, such as Reiki or meditation, relaxes your body and mind at the same time. Finding a good support group helps you find your voice and speak your truth. When women gather, there is a collective power to heal, find our voice, rise, and make a difference. Support groups provide a safe space for women to trust, love, dream and share—like-minded women supporting women without judgment.

As I gaze at that beautiful woman in the mirror, I see a woman who has completed a great deal of internal work healing herself. I have learned to love myself from the inside out. People are drawn to me because of my compassion, and they see me as the lighthouse in the storm, always surviving. Now, I am thriving, filled with passion and desire, and a love only I can provide for myself. I am being the change I want to see. Knowing that I am worthy and deserve to be loved and cherished, just as I am at this exact moment, attracts people into my life who are working on their inner trauma and no longer in the "victim mentality." People with a victim mentality feel as though terrible things keep happening and the world is against them. Those thought patterns changed as I rewired my mental attitude. A saying I use any time I start to spiral out of control is, "All of my life comes to me with ease and joy and glory." It is a saying from a course I attended called Access Consciousness. Sometimes, I repeat it twenty times to pull my thoughts back to this moment. The shift allowed me to recognize I needed to come first. My mental and physical health were my priority and only I could make the changes that were necessary for me to survive and move forward in my life.

The reflection in the mirror shows an accomplished author of eight books. I have shared stories of abuse and how I survived, encouraging women to heal their trauma. I teach people how to open to spirituality and find their life purpose, and I encourage them to choose new paths to help them heal, and, in turn, help others heal. I see a woman who broke the rules of what society defines a woman's role should be, by raising children and going back to high school at the same time to complete my grade 12 education. I would drive one child to daycare, drop the other one off at elementary school, and then drive myself to high school. Some days it was extremely difficult managing my household, completing homework, studying for tests, writing exams, and giving my children the love and attention they needed. As a single mother, it was a lot to juggle. The financial worries and stress from lack of resources, weekly counselling sessions, and an impending court case were too much for me. My brothers had molested my children. The Royal Canadian

Mounted Police (RCMP) had no record of the abuse I had endured as a child, and as a result, I had to retell my story and relive the trauma. I would sit in my bedroom at night and cry myself to sleep so the children couldn't see or hear me. I was devastated and blamed myself for not protecting them from their trauma. I was on the honor roll in the first semester of school, but I struggled to pass the second semester. Thankfully, the RCMP constable recommended group therapy, and I began the healing journey that would bring me to where I am today.

Instead of continuing with my education, I followed my parents' advice and obtained my class 1 license and drove long haul and short haul, by myself, in a male-dominated career. My farming background provided me with skills to drive and backup equipment and I was not afraid to get dirty! There were many pros and cons to being a single white female driving a semi-truck and trailer. One of the biggest pros was driving through and being a tourist in the United States from the West Coast to the East Coast and from the Canadian West Coast to Montreal. The biggest con was lying about having a male partner sleeping in the bunk when I stopped for fuel or food. Male truck drivers would try to "pick me up" or ask me to drive with them as a team driver. I was always looking over my shoulder, making sure I was not being followed, and ensuring my doors were locked as soon as I was back in the truck. I rarely ate in restaurants or spent time in truck stops, preferring the rest areas and the fridge and microwave in my truck. Safety was always my number one priority. I will admit my ego enjoyed the venture as well. I could back up a rig and park straighter than some of the male drivers out there! It was an experience that added to my journey.

Driving was not enough to push the limits of female societal norms, so I decided to build a house in a community that quashed women's growth and power. A second skill acquired from living on the farm was carpentry. It was another love-hate experience. I would call businesses for construction material pricing and also get a male coworker to call. His price was always cheaper so I would quote it when I picked up the material. My friends and coworkers helped me build the house. My parents never set foot in it and discouraged me from taking on such a huge project. I had dragged around the bag of disapproval from my parents my entire life and at this point, I no longer sought their approval or help. The more I healed myself, the stronger I became in learning what was best for me and who supported me on my journey.

Eventually, I circled back to my education path and attended university at 44 years old. I struggled to pass some of my classes, spending hours on essays and studying for tests to achieve a 60 percent grade. Through this process, I discovered I had a learning disability that stemmed from childhood seizures. This information led me to career counselling, which showed me new techniques for studying and taking notes. I was so proud of myself for finishing my first year with a 70 percent honor roll grade! I encountered some amazing women that year and wrote a book called, *I Survived So Can You*. Several of these amazing women submitted stories of traumas they had endured, and we celebrated our successes by publishing a book that explained how we survived and regained our personal power.

I continued to break the societal norms of women by buying a motorcycle, passing my class 6 driver's license, and riding by myself. At 57 years old, I jumped out of a plane at 10,000 feet to experience skydiving. What an adrenaline rush that was! I challenged my fears of water by white-water rafting and obtaining my Canadian Boating License. I've also learned how to ride a sea doo and drive a boat across the lake. I've owned successful businesses and employed disadvantaged women, empowering them with management roles and helping them complete apprenticeship hours.

When I look at my reflection, I see a woman who has weathered many storms and stands in the sunshine, glowing and basking in her personal power. The road has been long with many curves, hills, valleys, bumps, and side roads. However, it has brought me to this exact moment, gazing at the beautiful woman looking back at me in the mirror.

Melissa Mazurek

Melissa Mazurek is a passionate advocate for mental and emotional health, dedicated to the journey of self-discovery, self-love, healing and wholeness. As an intuitive, healer, and visionary, Melissa offers a unique, multidimensional approach to personal growth. She creates a safe and sacred space for others, supporting them as they tap into their inner power and wisdom.

Melissa's path has been marked by significant challenges, including childhood trauma, sexual abuse and assault, domestic violence, divorce, miscarriages, addiction, and suicidal tendencies. Despite these hardships, she has achieved a successful career as a financial controller and manager earning a six-figure salary before experiencing a profound breakdown that led to losing it all.

Today, Melissa's wisdom is deeply rooted in her lived experiences. She made the transformative decision to embark on her own healing journey, release the past, and embody the change she wishes to see in the world. Melissa now lives authentically, guided by her truth, beautiful heart, and resilient soul, offering hope and guidance to those ready to heal and thrive.

Melissa's purpose for writing in this book is to let others know they are not alone and that even when they feel like there is no way out, there is a way IN.

Connect with Melissa:

https://linktr.ee/melissa.mazurek

Chapter 11

If Only I Had Known: The Journey Back Home to Myself

By Melissa Dawn Mazurek

Never did I imagine that the first half of my life would be filled with uncertainty, chaos, abuse, and trauma, which resulted in struggles with my mental, emotional, and physical well-being. I wanted to take care of everyone around me, to make sure others were OK. I was doing my best to show affection—giving gifts and letting others know they were loved—while also growing in my career. These were the areas I focused on until I found myself on my bathroom floor fighting for my life.

When I close my eyes and reflect on my earliest memory, deep down in my heart, I feel I was meant to come into this world to LOVE—to love my family and everyone else. I just wanted to love. Even though you hear the phrase, "To love others, you must love yourself first," I realized I did not know how to do this, nor did I fully comprehend the importance of this until now. Who teaches us these things? Our dear parents? From what I witnessed in mine, they did not know how to do that for themselves, so how could they teach me? I remember telling myself in my younger years, along with my siblings, that "I would never be like them." Oh, the irony.

I learned at an early age that something was "off" in my world. What I was living through and experiencing at home was not what I was witnessing or hearing about happening to others. I had a few friends who could relate to some things, but I felt it was not to the extent of what was happening to me. My home life and family dynamic were not ideal. It was chaotic, volatile, uncertain, and unsafe. At some point in my childhood, I had unconsciously made it my mission to try to love and save my family.

From this young age, I began empathizing and literally feeling the pain of my mother, father, siblings, and others. I remember thinking, "If they just felt love maybe they wouldn't suffer so much." This would be the beginning of the savior, martyr, fixer, good girl, and other self-sacrificing patterns I would carry through the rest of my life. I experienced unhealthy relationships that would affect my well-being, eventually risking almost losing my life and everything I had worked so hard for.

An area of my life I excelled in was my job and career. I started coping with what was happening at home in my younger years by getting my first job at thirteen. Shortly after that, I worked at two places and attended school. So, excelling in my career was something I had much pride in. I worked for great people at an oilfield company, making a salary of close to six figures. I bought my second house on my own. I drove a beautiful vehicle. I travelled two to three times a year. I would do what I thought would bring me moments of relief and joy from the other areas of my life that weren't going so well. Eventually, coping with work and trying to escape my reality caught up with me. My trauma symptoms would keep getting worse as more traumatic experiences happened in my life. Old coping strategies no longer worked, and I found myself trying to do whatever it took to cope. This led me down a path where I had no other choice but to likely lose my life or find a different way out of the pain and suffering I was in. I had sacrificed my mental and emotional well-being for my career. I was advised by my doctor to stop working two weeks before my employers called me in for a meeting to discuss what they were observing with me and my well-being and how it was now affecting my ability to do my job. I finally handed in the letter from my doctor and my leave from my career commenced.

Going back to me laying on my bathroom floor, pleading with myself and God to make it through—this ultimately led me down a deep healing journey. It was a journey back home to myself, to the person I never truly knew. Oh, but I know her now, and never could I have imagined that all my experiences that took me to my knees would now, in hindsight, be my biggest teachers. This is what I know now that I wish I had known then: You can literally come back from anything. You don't know what you don't know, so give yourself grace. We can decide to take the time to learn and go within in order to do differently. If you think about it, making a one-degree adjustment, though it seems small, can actually change the trajectory of your life.

Pain can be the biggest catalyst for change.

There is nothing wrong with me or you. Whatever your symptoms are or however your emotions are coming out is exactly as they are meant to since they are based on the experiences you've had and the conditioning you have received. They are meant to be listened to. The answers we need are within the pain. Most of us have not been taught how to process our emotions, and since childhood, have been taught to suppress or to ignore what our emotions or bodies are telling us. There is wisdom in it all, in how we relate to our emotions, labeling them as right or wrong. We are not our emotions; we are merely the observer of them.

Emotions are energy. Energy needs to move. This means we need to fully feel our emotions so they are not suppressed in our bodies which causes energy blocks and can lead to "dis-ease." I can speak from experience as when I was no longer able to work, I was diagnosed with major depressive disorder, multiple anxiety disorders, and complex post-traumatic stress disorder. My assessment came back 55/21, which is more than double the "score" needed to be considered "disabled/diagnosed." I also found out that I had Fibromyalgia and hyperinflated lungs after going in to get my heart checked. I now realize it was due to holding my breath most of my life, which stems from trauma. I could barely walk up a flight of stairs. I did not understand why my body was being so affected in my mid-thirties, so I researched and learned how trauma affects your nervous system, brain and energy. I refused to stay there. I was determined to heal. Though I did not know how long it would take but I was not going to give up. To help others, I realized I would need to learn to do it for myself first. This would be my initiation.

I have come to know earth as a school. I believe we come here to have experiences that allow us to evolve and grow. We integrate the lessons and expand our perspectives to understand ourselves and others, leading us to be more accepting. Earth is a planet of duality and polarity. My research into Universal Laws helped me understand how the energies and consciousness work. This helped change my perspective of always feeling like life was happening to me, and like I was hopeless and powerless to understand even the energetics behind some of my experiences.

When I finally left my first abusive relationship, which took me a long time to leave, I wondered how I could have let this happen. I witnessed my mom being abused my entire childhood and I always said I would never let a man treat me that way. I began judging and shaming myself because of what I had witnessed in my past and society about being a victim. But instead of letting myself be a victim of abuse, I took responsibility for what was happening to me. In taking on that responsibility, I then became my own abuser without even realizing it.

They say, "Life can only be understood backward, but it must be lived forward." The lesson I see in my abusive relationships is that they were providing me an opportunity to learn how to love myself. My abusers were showing me a reflection of how I had been making choices that would not reflect that I loved and valued myself. "As within, so without." I didn't see until later that the pattern of trying to love people who were experiencing their own pain and hurting me as a child stemmed from the subconscious programming I received in my upbringing. I would try to love and help my parents in whatever way I could, including stepping in front of my mother and being willing to be physically harmed so that her spouse would stop harming her. I sacrificed myself in an attempt to save others. My heart broke all over again when I realized how I was harming myself, unintentionally and unconsciously. I had to see it, otherwise, how would I know what to change or where to begin?

Your brain does not know the difference between a thought and an experience. So, if we think about a traumatic experience or create a story in our mind, our brain and body will react and create the biochemistry within our body, such as stress hormones, as if we were currently living the experience. This is another reason why it's important to be aware of our thoughts and stories. What I also realized is that the first ten years of therapy were mostly talk therapy, and retelling my story repeatedly actually kept me in a cycle of retraumatizing myself. While it's important to tell our story and have it be witnessed and validated, trauma does not get healed in our minds. We must feel it to heal from it.

What We Know Now

A big "a-ha" moment in my healing journey came from realizing that I hadn't allowed myself to be a victim of abuse, preventing me from truly healing and leaving me powerless. I searched for the answers outside of myself. Without the validation from my parents growing up, I did not know how to validate myself. The process of reparenting myself began after I learned the tools needed to be calm and self-regulate. This allowed me to become more aware and identify what I was feeling emotionally and where I was feeling it within my body. Once I allowed myself to grieve—to feel anger and sadness—and acknowledge the many horrible things that happened in my life, only then was I able to find safety within myself. When we do not validate our pain or have someone else validate it, we are rejecting our truth. If you reject your truth, then you will never feel safe within your own body or mind. I became my own savior. I want to make it clear that you must allow yourself to be the victim, but the process is very much incomplete if you do not come out of the victim state. I say this because when we are a victim, we are not in our power and that is OK. However, there needs to be a step taken to say, "I'm taking back my power and bringing it back into you as your responsibility." The quote that comes to mind here is, "Trauma is not your fault, but you are responsible for your healing."

Being triggered and reactive only reflected the pain and trauma that had been suppressed and stored within my body. If we avoid the feelings we label as right or wrong then what we resist will persist and come out sideways, not in a reactive way but as a chosen response. What I wish for others to know is that judging yourself for your reactions will put you into a state of defensiveness, and back into a fight-or-flight response, which is like your brain being hijacked and not your authentic self. So, creating a judgment on yourself for your behavior without knowing or understanding yourself will create another wound. This is why practicing compassion and grace for yourself is especially important. Take a moment to reflect here. Take a few deep breaths into your heart and reflect on how you treat yourself when you make a mistake. Are you compassionate or do you criticize yourself and do the tough love thing? Does your heart feel more open when you criticize yourself or does your heart feel open when you give yourself love and compassion? I was raised to be tougher than my emotions and in turn, I believed how I felt was wrong. This led to me feeling more shame and repeating the pattern. When we shame others for having emotions that make us uncomfortable, we are suppressing them rather than holding space for them. Free yourself! Become the person (parent) you need or once needed. I look at myself as having my soul (my inner child), my masculine (my inner father), and my feminine (my inner mother).

Our subconscious is what runs the show. The subconscious mind is the part of the brain that we are not aware of, yet it influences our actions and feelings. This is where our "Shadow" lives. The "Shadow" is any part of you that you do not see, acknowledge, or accept. Our subconscious is around ninety-five percent of our mind. This is why it's important to take the time to go into the subconscious, bring it into our conscious awareness, and reprogram what is not working for ourselves, including limiting beliefs and conditioning from our parents, family, friends, schools, TV/movies, billboards, and songs that we didn't even realize we had absorbed. Our subconscious mind is constantly being programmed, scanning, and receiving messages from our environments. The environments we surround ourselves with matter.

What We Know Now

Your feelings have the answers within them. It is how we relate to our emotions that can change it all. Be inquisitive, notice the discomfort in your body, the tightening of your jaw or your stomach, and the breath you are holding—they are signals that your body is trying to communicate with you. Ask it what it feels, and what it wants to say, and listen. When we are not in acceptance, we are in resistance, and we create suffering. For example, if you deny you are hurt or in pain, you will continue to suffer.

Our triggers are there to show us where we are not yet free. It's an opportunity to heal and take our power back. What triggers us about others is often because they express a part of themselves that we have shamed and disowned within. When we cannot sit with ourselves and our emotions, we cannot be with others in theirs.

We are spiritual beings having a human experience. We are here to evolve. "A miracle is a change in perspective." I have now been able to look backward as the observer of my life and see it through new eyes, a new perspective that has liberated me.

"You will cry tears of joy and gratitude when you realize that your healing journey was the path home to yourself."

What I once was so desperate to receive from others—to be seen, to be witnessed, to be believed, to be protected, to be cared for, and to be loved—I am now able to give this to myself, for myself. This is the greatest gift I have ever given myself.

You are Your Own Greatest Healer

Poem written by Melissa Dawn Mazurek

With every ounce of my soul

I breathe in and out

Giving myself permission

To let it all go

Feeling the discomfort

Of where I've been

Knowing there is a freedom

Coming from within

As I remember, who I really am

I rise like a phoenix

My power igniting within

The flames of the fire freeing me

From the illusions that were still held in

From the ashes, I rise

Stronger than I have ever been.

Shona Welsh

Shona Welsh, founder of Speak Easy with Shona Welsh, is passionate about helping others claim their confidence and has enjoyed coaching leaders on effectively communicating with a global workforce in five countries. Shona was the first female executive when she joined an international corporation early in her career. She has served as a non-profit executive director, communication specialist/speech writer for Canadian elected officials, and has also led successful public sector change initiatives. With numerous international clients, Shona designs/facilitates communication programs for several UN agencies and leads a renowned Middle Eastern public speaking program. Eighty percent of her communication graduates are promoted within one year, her clients regularly place in the top three in speaking contests, and her teams win a high percentage of bid presentations.

Shona holds a master's degree in adult learning and numerous professional communication, HR, and innovation certifications. She has published 12 books, won numerous speaking and writing awards, and can't be left alone in the house with chocolate.

Connect with Shona:
https://linktr.ee/shonawelsh

Chapter 12

Claiming My Confidence
Overcoming Perpetual People-Pleasing

By Shona Welsh

I was super irritated.

A friend had recently spent weeks venting to me about a conference she was organizing with a colleague who refused to hear her ideas and was a control freak about everything. Armed with a strategy we created, she was determined to advocate for herself—and then immediately folded in the face of her colleague's refusal to budge. In the end, she capitulated to all her colleague's wishes. While they ultimately received great feedback and I was happy for her, I was confused by my underlying irritation. So, I spent a few hours getting curious.

It turns out my irritation came from three sources:

1. Exasperation at my friend for allowing herself to be bulldozed (and then making it worse by telling me she'd be willing to do it again!)
2. Annoyance at all the times I've seen smart, educated, capable women do the same thing.
3. Anger at myself for being guilty of all of it.

This kind of people-pleasing is nothing new to women, whether it's in romance, friendship, or workplace relationships. There's nothing wrong with being kind and wanting to make others happy. The act of helping others is one of the greatest pleasures of our lives.

But many women struggle with taking that too far by not saying "no" and sacrificing their own needs to avoid conflict or discomfort. Regardless of religion, culture, and parents, women are still socialized as nurturers in relationships. We're seen as caretakers in almost all cultures, whether we have children or not.

Awareness of my own people-pleasing was a key revelation from my second divorce. Even though I was heading into all the challenges of single parenting, my life actually got *easier* because I had one less needy person to care for. I had spent a lot of time making my husband's life easy at the expense of my own happiness. I was the only person working, delivering and picking up my son from daycare daily, making dinner the minute I got home, playing with and putting my son to bed every evening, and then studying and writing papers late into the night in pursuit of my graduate degree. Oh, and I got to do all the housework and laundry in my "spare" moments. By the time we split, I'd been asking myself for a while, "What the heck do I need a husband for?"

At its heart, people-pleasing is an effort to prove our worth. Fear is the underlying emotion—fear that you're not good enough, that others will reject or abandon you, and that they will withdraw affection and approval. The result is often relentlessly putting your own needs and desires last. And as I learned the hard way, you can only do that for so long before you rebel. When that rebellion comes, it's frequently life-altering.

I come from a lengthy line of coal miners stuck in a class system that had forever held them down. My parents envisioned a better life for my sister and me, and we moved to Canada when I was five years old. Like many children of immigrant parents, I was indoctrinated with the belief that "education is everything." So, I overachieved. Regularly. Straight A report cards were your ticket to success.

Heaven forbid anything bad be on your permanent record! This continued after high school. I wasn't sure what I wanted to do but was forced to attend university immediately following graduation. No gap year for me. That was for losers.

In my first year, I brought home a failing grade in one course and was confined to home for the summer. Yep, I was a legal adult, albeit a new one, but was shamed and bullied into reflecting for months on this significant failure. Surely this was the gateway to a life of poverty, heroin addiction, and *gasp*, being a two-time divorcee. In fairness, my parents didn't connect the course failure to the two divorces… that came later. Nope. Those were clearly about my faulty character. I could have easily passed the course—I just didn't go to class, despite the consequences I knew awaited me. What I didn't realize at the time was that this failure was the first stirring of an inner rebellion that had been heating up for years. It would take another 10 of them for me to finally reach a full boil.

After university, I embarked on an overachieving career consistent with my upbringing, attaining all my parents' required measures of success. Before I turned 35, I rose to executive ranks and won numerous speech contests and other awards. I was the first person in my entire extended family to earn a master's degree. I published several best-selling books and started a successful business.

None of it was good enough for my parents because my personal life was in shambles. I needed to be perfect in *every* area of life, and until I was, I would remain an underperformer in their eyes. My mother's favorite comment was, "You're not very good at relationships, are you?"

When I got married the first time, my relationship was a carbon copy of my parental one. He told me what to do, I did it and spent most of my time stuffing my resentment down to keep the peace. It's not a unique story. We tend to repeat the relationships we grow up with. A few months into my first marriage, I was diagnosed with early-stage cervical cancer. I remember waking up from a successful surgery thinking, "Would I be happy with my life if I died today?" My inner voice whispered quietly but clearly: "No."

Rebellion #1: Leaving my first husband after one year

My parents didn't like him but still viewed our divorce as a failure. No one had *ever* been divorced in our family. What would they tell the relatives back home? Thank God your grandparents are gone.

Enter husband #2. My mom and dad didn't like him either. This one lasted a few years longer but ended for similar reasons. In the last year of our marriage, I would frequently awake after vivid, angry dreams featuring my parents and husband. It would take me a while to calm my intense emotions. While I told myself they were only dreams, I began questioning why their frequency was increasing. The final year of our marriage included the removal of my gall bladder after numerous excruciating attacks.

Finding myself in a hospital recovery room once again, my inner voice moved from whisper to shout: "One bout of cancer and now organ removal. What are you willing to experience next before you choose the life *you* want?"

Rebellion #2: Ending my second marriage

"Where have we gone wrong?" my parents lamented, absorbing my shame as their own. Worse, I had a son this time. How would it affect him coming from a broken home? Never mind that his father had been largely absent from his daily life since birth (six weeks after my husband and I split, my 4-year-old finally noticed he was gone).

Rebellion #3: A year of intense self-reflection

This might not seem like rebellion to most people, but to my parents, it was a waste of time and a surrender to "psychological mumbo jumbo." In their eyes, its only purpose was to allow me to excuse myself from being a failure. "Focus on raising your son," my parents said (as if I wasn't already). "Remember, relationships aren't your thing."

Luckily, my inner voice remained loud and clear, but this time with a gentle honesty that was new to me: "There's a common denominator in all your relationships—and it's you. Why do you keep making these choices?" You'll notice I didn't say "bad" choices. I was determined to frame my exploration objectively and without judgment. My whole life—both professional and personal—had been an effort to please my parents, to turn myself into something that would make *them* happy and have *them* think I was a success.

As I became an adult, I saw the world as a place where I needed to focus on what made my husband and my bosses happy. I didn't stand up for myself in many situations where I should have. I was smart, well-educated, and capable—just like my friend who so irritated me because she gave in to her colleague—and yet, I buried my own wishes and wants in service of everyone else's.

After my year of self-study, it was time to step into a new life of claiming my confidence. I won't tell you it's always been a smooth road, but it's been a much happier one. Instead of rebelling, I was now embracing opportunities that felt authentic for *me*, regardless of the disapproval of my parents and others.

Opportunity #1: Husband #3

The absolute last thing I wanted in the world was to get married again. I was still tentative about the new me, and romance was most definitely not on my radar.

Not surprisingly, my parents didn't like Husband #3. They threw a massive fit.

"He comes from a different religion! He's a divorcee with three teenagers! How can you let him raise your son?!" I quietly stated that he treated me with respect, love, and kindness, noting that we never argued and calmly discussed issues as true partners should. The pressure was relentless, but I was determined to trust my heart. We're still together after 26 years.

Opportunity #2: Child #2

If another husband wasn't on my radar, another child wasn't even in the same universe. We were already in the middle of the complex process of blending our two families of three teenagers and a 5-year-old. But while our daughter was a startling surprise, she was ultimately a welcome one. I knew that if I could love my son as much as I did, then I could love another child in the same way.

Upon learning the news of my pregnancy, my parents turned up the emotional blackmail heat by cutting me out of the family. It was among the most painful times in my life, but I knew the alternative was to go back to who I was. And there was no way I was doing that. My blended, extended family became a true source of strength for me. My husband and I did everything as full partners, with lots of communication and understanding. His family was kind and loving, accepting my son from the very beginning as their brother, nephew, and grandchild.

To this day, the five siblings never refer to each other as "half this" or "step that." They're siblings. That's it.

Opportunity #3: Starting a business

The challenges and growth in my personal life gave me a new view of my professional life. I came to realize that my overachievement tendencies, while positive and motivating in some respects, also led to overwork, burnout, and at times, mental health challenges. The more I began identifying what *I* really wanted, the less I felt at home in my work roles. I chose a career in training and development because I genuinely like and am interested in people—and that hasn't changed. What *did* change was my willingness to go along with dysfunctional and even toxic corporate cultures. So, I started my own business.

My parents, who had reinstated contact after our daughter was born, threw yet another fit. "How could I leave a respectable job? What if things failed? You have too many mouths to feed!"

That was 20 years ago. I won't tell you there haven't been lean times and other challenges because there have been many! But the bills are always paid, every mouth is always fed, and more importantly, everyone is happy, including me.

***

In the years since my parents have been gone, I have come to see them as the deeply wounded survivors of war and class discrimination, and as the rigid social rule followers that they were. Their intentions were good, if misguided, and they did the best they could with the tools they were given. While I can't tell you that we ever regained the close relationship of my childhood, in the last years of their lives, we found a way to have a mostly pleasant, if superficial, relationship.

Despite everything, I can't tell you I've completely overcome my people-pleasing tendencies. It continues to be a work in progress, and I suspect it will be until the end of my life. Curing yourself of people-pleasing is a journey of self-discovery, self-honesty, and quite frankly, bravery. Some days, I'm braver than others.

I still sometimes doubt that I'm reading certain situations correctly.

I still sometimes question if I have a right to feel offended by certain behaviors.

And I still sometimes worry that I will alienate people with my choices.

What I can tell you is that I'm able to identify those feelings as soon as they arise and make a conscious decision to override them. It's not always easy, but I'm committed to never again allowing people-pleasing to be my default.

One of the biggest challenges for women is living in a world surrounded by airbrushed versions of what they should look like, live like, and be like, no matter how they were raised. I was determined that my daughters wouldn't succumb to the same "not good enough" self-view that plagued me. While growing up is filled with the regular assortment of challenging and sometimes dysfunctional "situationships," it's incredibly gratifying that through all of it, both have remained confident in themselves. I've watched them stand their ground through multiple personal and professional challenges while staying true to their own convictions about who they are and what they want.

As for my sons, while they've had their own struggles with feeling inadequate at times, they've all grown into thoughtful, caring men. We have amazing conversations about life, love, and navigating their own difficulties with finding their place in a world where male roles are changing. They've also brought a collection of smart, strong, and confident daughters-in-law into our family of which I am deeply proud. All of them are passing down a legacy of confidence and self-worth to our grandchildren.

In the end, this is the greatest gift of my journey: Breaking a generational legacy of people-pleasing so my children and grandchildren are free to be themselves.

Susie De Giusti

Susie De Giusti is a woman committed to living boldly and authentically, with a mission to help women overcome their limiting beliefs and fearlessly embrace the opportunities before them. Having spent years on her own personal growth journey, Susie understands that real change doesn't happen overnight. Even now, as she approaches her sixties, she faces life's challenges and continues to navigate them on her terms. She believes in the power of learning, growing, and granting oneself the grace to evolve and make necessary changes, even from past mistakes. By doing so, Susie embodies the possibility of living a life that is bold and uniquely authentic.

Aside from being the CEO and founder of TGIF—Towards Gainful Infinite Freedom Inc., Susie is also a life coach, author, speaker, and the visionary behind Gentle Whispers Retreat. Beyond her professional accomplishments, she is known for being a loving daughter and the primary caregiver to her mother, understanding firsthand the profound challenges of being a parent's caregiver. In her rare moments of solitude, Susie enjoys reading, crafting, walking in nature, and taking well-deserved naps. Above all, she cherishes breaking bread with family and friends, creating memories that always bring a smile to her face.

Connect with Susie:

Susie De Giusti | Instagram, Facebook | Linktree

Chapter 13

Finding Grace Amid Life's Shittiest Moments

By Susie De Giusti

Shit happens for a reason! And it continues to happen until we get the lesson. Let me share with you here how shit happened to me.

The year 2011 was a year of change for me. It started with me attending Choices, a personal development course. I needed clarity on why my life wasn't going as I hoped and prayed it would. Why was I so depressed and secretly angry at the world? I walked out of that seminar understanding myself better, about who I am and why I am the way I am. Stripping back the layers was brutal yet necessary to get to where I am today. At one point that same year, I dismissed the lessons and sat in my murky water of "Why is shit always happening to me?" I'm a good person, loving, caring, and considerate. I wear my heart on my sleeve, and yet nothing seems to go right.

Have you ever had an event that made you question everything in your life? Do you ever look back on that event and wish you had known more about the situation or how NOT to have the situation occur? I do!

I was driving to work one beautiful sunny summer morning in 2011. I was late, as usual. Traffic was piled up, though for no apparent reason, and I was feeling frustrated. I hated everything about getting to work, and really hated the fact that with all the good that I've been doing, I was not receiving the same in return. Ever feel this way? I don't know what put me in such a foul mood—perhaps hormones, self-pity, or both… who knows! I found myself screaming in despair as I sat behind that steering wheel, without a care in the world if the fellow driver next to me witnessed my madness. Thankfully, I somehow made it through the day and was eager to meet my friend, Kerry, and rush off to a lovely dinner before catching the production of *Wicked* at the Jubilee Auditorium. It would be a great evening, or so I thought.

I was taking a left-hand turn, and between the sun and a blind spot, I did not see the car coming in the far-right lane. BANG! Shaken, shocked and confused, I saw nothing but smoke from the airbags in front of me.

"Kerry, are you OK?" I asked.

"What just happened? Why is the car smoking and where are my glasses?"

"Kerry, are you OK?" I asked again.

"Yes. Why is the car smoking?" I had to ask her to get out of the car in case there was a small fire. Her glasses landed on the floor. She picked them up, put them on, and we both exited the car. I was shaking and on the verge of tears when I approached the other car to ensure the driver and passengers were alright. Thankfully, no one was injured. The driver was a kind man who reassured me that everyone was fine as I started to sob, realizing that it could have been a LOT worse than what it was. When I think about it, had I turned one second sooner than I did, rather than the front end of the car being struck, the passenger car door would have taken the hit and Kerry would not have been OK.

While waiting for the responders, I walked around crying in shock and disbelief while continuously checking with everyone and their well-being. A witness to the accident was staying close to me as she was afraid that I would fall or faint from the shock I was in. That beautiful soul was reliving her own trauma, thanks to my stupidity. She had shared that her friend passed away at that same intersection in a similar accident not long ago. This only led me to cry harder, apologizing to her for causing the pain in reliving the event.

Every single person, other than me, was calm and easygoing. The driver of the other car, assuring me that everything was fine, said, "Accidents happen, that's why we have insurance." They were so calm, patient and kind. I was waiting for someone to yell at me and tell me how stupid and careless I was… anything to justify how I felt. Responders arrived and the cleanup began. Statements were given, and insurance information was swapped. I stayed behind with the officer, who should have fined me more than they did (it was the right fine, I just felt I needed more of a lashing), while Kerry headed home to get her car. Fortunately, we were only a few blocks from her place.

I knew there was no way I could sit through *Wicked* with a sound mind or in physical comfort. I did not walk away unscathed from the accident; I had quite a few large bruises. So, with that, Kerry, her mom, and I headed to the Jubilee Auditorium to see if we could swap our tickets for another evening. I explained what happened to the box office attendant, asking to exchange tickets for another day. I was told curtly, "NO," with no apology, and that exchanges were not allowed. I could feel the tears well up again when, out of the blue, this angel standing next to me confronted the attendant for being rude and inconsiderate of what I had just gone through. She insisted that the attendant speak to her manager and figure something out. Before I knew it, I was given a contact number and instructions to call the next day to get new dates for the show. I turned to thank the lady, but she was nowhere to be seen! POOF, gone in the wind. You know when you watch movies and the character is standing there looking around and the camera does a blurred 360-degree scan of the scenery, while the person standing looks dazed and in wonder? That was me at that moment. My guardian angel came and went, and I was not able to thank her personally.

That day had begun with me in a rage, yet it ended in sorrow… and a blessing. Never have I felt so grateful for how things ended, considering it could have been much worse. I thanked every angel, guardian, God, Jesus, and Mother Mary. I sobbed the remainder of the evening, feeling unworthy of forgiveness or kindness to be shown my way. I was brilliant at beating myself up. At one point, my mom had to remind me that the stress I was putting on myself would not help my situation, as I was in the "two-week wait" phase of my in vitro procedure. You see, at the time, I was trying to get pregnant, and I will never know if I was. The stress I went through that day and the recovery from the accident was not in my favor. My chances of being pregnant were slim to none.

I look back on that day knowing I was not using the tools I learned at the Choices seminar to make my day the best I could, regardless of outside circumstances. I threw all the lessons out the window when I rushed to work. Despite being armed with these tools, I was oblivious to the fact that my thoughts, feelings, and actions were not in alignment that day. There is such a gap between what we know and what we do. Rather than building that bridge to connect what we know and do, we often find ourselves in the ditch, splashing around in the murky waters. I was not in control of myself that rage-filled morning in 2011 and because of it, I let the unfolding of shit happen.

Shit happens because we are not paying attention to what is going on, on the inside of our being. Our focus is consumed by outside circumstances and how we view them. Life throws us curveballs and we can lose sight of the bigger picture. But the truth is, the shitty moments can teach us the greatest lessons, if we're willing to pay attention. This is why I'm sharing my story with you... I don't want you to go through fits and scares and learn the hard way.

Let's be real for a minute—just because we've taken a course or read a book on self-help doesn't mean we're suddenly experts at improving ourselves. The harsh truth is that reading about change and actually making it happen are two completely different things. Too often, we get caught up in the thrill of learning a new technique or strategy, only to let it collect dust on the shelf. We think simply absorbing the information is enough, but true personal growth requires consistent, dedicated effort.

Here are three easy steps you could take right now:

Step 1: Get honest with yourself! Look at where you are today and ask yourself if you are seeing your desired results. Get clear on what you want in life, and if you aren't exactly sure what that is, examine what you don't want. This could help you gain some clarity.

Step 2: Gain some perspective! You know how they say there are two sides to every story? The same idea can apply to your life. Try to view your life from different perspectives. On that day in 2011, I could only see what I was lacking in my life. I did not see what I had. I never considered what I wasn't doing to make life better.

Step 3: Practice awareness and understanding. Recognize the situation you are in and why. Sometimes, we allow things to happen subconsciously, and the reason why may not be clear. But with a bit of work and uncovering the layers, we can begin to see things differently and have a better understanding.

The reality is that self-improvement is a lifelong journey, not a quick fix. It's about developing the discipline to implement what we've learned and sticking to it, even when the going gets tough. Merely accumulating knowledge won't cut it. We must be willing to put in the hard work to transform our habits and behaviors. I'm not saying this to be discouraging. My mission is to empower you to approach self-improvement with a renewed sense of purpose and accountability. But I also want you to know that each of our timelines will be different for the transformation to appear.

It took me almost a decade AFTER that accident to FULLY understand that my knowing and doing state of mind were not aligned and I needed to make further changes.

What do I mean by this?

Have you ever felt stuck or like you are on a hamster wheel and not getting anywhere? While you know how to get yourself out of the situation, you procrastinate and struggle to change. This gap between our knowing and our doing is a real and pervasive challenge that many of us face. Surprisingly, our educational system doesn't place more emphasis on bridging this divide and empowering students to translate their knowledge into meaningful action, making it easier for all of us as we become adults. The truth is that our thoughts and feelings have a profound impact on the outcomes we experience in life. It's not about karma or the belief that good deeds will automatically be rewarded. Rather, it's about understanding the power of our mindset and the actions we choose to take. I chose to be in a rage, and have my feelings dictate my outcome.

It may be tempting to try to simply think positive thoughts, hoping that will lead to the results you desire. However, the reality is that your feelings and vibrations play a crucial role in the outcome.

If your underlying feelings are negative, and you're trying to think positively on the surface, the summation of both your positivity and negativity will ultimately determine your outcome—not precisely what you want but not that bad either. Have you experienced a day when you felt great, like on a high, yet fully conscious of your surroundings, and everything turned up rosy? Your body was likely emitting positive vibrations and when that happens, your results are exactly as you want or better. On the flip side, if you're experiencing a day feeling gloomy, short-tempered, and overreacting to everything, your body is then emitting negative vibrations and your results are equally the same… shit. That shit continues until you change your state.

Your vibrations, which reflect your dominant thoughts and emotions, act as a magnet, attracting circumstances and experiences that match that frequency. Positive vibrations will draw in positive results, while negative vibrations will attract more of what you don't want. When we find ourselves facing challenges or obstacles, it's crucial that we take a step back and honestly assess where our focus has been. Are we dwelling on the negative and allowing our emotions to dictate our behavior? Or are we proactively directing our attention and energy towards constructive solutions and empowering ourselves to make positive changes?

The gap between knowing and doing can only be bridged through a combination of self-awareness, discipline, and a willingness to step out of our comfort zones. It requires us to take a hard look at the "shit that happens" in our lives and take responsibility for our role in creating those circumstances. By shifting our mindset and aligning our actions with our deepest values and aspirations, we unlock the true potential for transformation. It's not always easy, but the rewards are immeasurable. Imagine the impact you could have on your life, your relationships, and the world around you if you were able to consistently bridge that knowing-doing gap.

I cannot remember why I was so angry that fateful day in 2011, but I did learn that I wasn't acknowledging what was happening inside of me—those feelings, where were they coming from?

Other lessons I learned were:

- I can't control what is beyond my power.
- My self-improvement journey is ongoing.
- I need to give more priority to my self-care and address my physical, emotional, and mental health needs.
- It is okay to be vulnerable and ask for help.
- I should learn to say "No" occasionally. I don't always need to do everything for everyone else.
- I am human. I make mistakes and should show myself compassion.
- Silver linings can be found in every lesson.
- And the biggest lesson… life doesn't happen *to* you; it happens *with* you!

I wish I had known all this much sooner and at a younger age. I can only imagine that I would be further ahead today, but alas, as per my last lesson learned, life was happening with me. I've made decisions, taken matters into my own hands, and have not allowed the outside world to dominate my life. I don't rely on a "job" to pay my way; I created a business that makes me thrive in my purpose to help you, my reader, live a kickass life! I laugh and smile more. I do what I want and when I want, all the while caring for my aging mama. I'm breaking the mold of what is expected of me as a woman.

I am the CEO of my own company, author, life coach, and speaker, and living my best life.

I can look back at the car accident and give thanks for it today. It was the beginning of learning about how thoughts and feelings can move me to attain the results I want. Kerry and I can both giggle a bit at how Kerry was confused, as she should have been, in asking why the car was smoking and what happened to her glasses. We see it like it was a movie today. She was the one who lightened the moment with her goofy way.

The way I see it, life is what we make of it. We may not be able to control every circumstance, but we can control how we respond to them. We can choose to be resilient, find the silver linings, and learn and grow from our experiences. The good news is, it's never too late to start. But we must be willing to get uncomfortable, challenge our old habits, and put in the consistent effort required to truly transform ourselves.

So, the next time you feel like life is just happening to you, take a step back and remember that you are the protagonist in your own story. You have the power to write the next chapter, to turn obstacles into opportunities, and to create the life you genuinely want to live. You are never alone on your journey! Women all over the world are uniting and supporting one another to evolve into the best versions of themselves. Step out and find the right group for you. Know that I am here to support you in any way I can, near or far.

Now, the choice is yours. Will you continue to let the gap between knowing and doing hold you back, or will you rise to the challenge to bridge the gap and embrace the idea that the life you are worthy and deserving of awaits you?

Conclusion

As we reach the final pages of *Echoes of Wisdom*, we are reminded of the enduring power of shared experiences. The 14 courageous women who bared their souls within these chapters have gifted us more than just stories—they have offered us their lessons, strength, and wisdom. In doing so, they have created a bond that transcends the pages of this book, a connection that resonates deeply with every woman who picks it up.

The journey through the trials of self-love, failed marriages, immigration, financial struggles, and battling cancer is not a linear one. Each story in this collection has shown that growth is rarely straightforward, and healing often comes from the most unexpected places. The wisdom imparted by these women is not the kind you acquire overnight. It is hard-earned, rooted in perseverance, and shaped by the strength that emerges when one chooses to rise after falling.

For the women who have walked a similar path, *Echoes of Wisdom* serves as a powerful reminder that you are not alone. In moments of self-doubt, heartbreak, or uncertainty, these stories stand as beacons of hope, illuminating the way forward. Whether you find yourself at the start of your journey or deep in the process of healing, the insights shared here are meant to guide you toward a deeper understanding of yourself and the strength that lies within.

For younger women, this book is a gift of foresight. The challenges that may seem insurmountable today are the very experiences that will shape the woman you will become tomorrow. As you read through the personal narratives in these pages, take with you the knowledge that adversity is not the end—it is an opportunity to rebuild, grow, and thrive. Let these stories serve as a reminder that even in the darkest moments, there is wisdom to be gained, and there is always a path forward.

The collective voices in *Echoes of Wisdom* remind us that our stories—however different they might be—are bound by universal themes of perseverance, hope, and self-discovery. Life may test us in various ways, but it is in how we respond to these tests that we find our true strength. Every challenge faced and overcome becomes a thread in the tapestry of our lives, weaving together a story of victory, growth, and, ultimately, wisdom.

As you close this book, may you carry with you the echoes of the voices within these pages. Let them inspire you to live boldly, love fiercely, and trust in your own journey. May the wisdom shared here remind you that, no matter where life takes you, you possess within yourself the courage to rise above any challenge and the strength to write your own story of resilience and self-love.

This is not the end, but a continuation—an invitation to embrace your own echoes of wisdom, and to pass them on to others, just as these women have done.

As a child, did you dream of being more? Maybe you imagined yourself singing, dancing on stage, becoming a world-renowned detective, or even teaching the next generation. But like so many of us, as time passed, those dreams faded under the weight of expectations from family and society. Sound familiar?

It took me until my 40s to realize something powerful: I always had the right to live life on my own terms. I wasn't taught this. Like many generations of women before me, I was conditioned to follow a path that wasn't truly mine.

But I learned that in order to live the life I was meant to, I needed to let go of old beliefs and societal standards. I had to create a new list of dreams that felt aligned with *me*. I learned to IMAGINE my life and live it in the way that is perfect for me.

You can do this too. We can be loving, nurturing women for our families **and** fiercely pursue our dreams. There is more than enough room for both. The only thing standing in your way is the old you.

Are you ready to embrace your full potential? It's time to rewrite your story, reclaim your dreams, and live a life that's entirely yours.

Join me on this journey to rediscover what it means to live fully — on your terms. Let's get started today.

Susie De Giusti

https://tgifreedom.life

27° Where Reality Embraces Your Dreams

Let your Voice be heard! Get the Edge You Need. A magazine that will connect you globally, help you build a community, collaborate with other businesswomen, and connect you with investors.

THE DETAILS

Welcome to 27°

The Business Lifestyle Magazine reached a diverse, global audience, offering unparalleled exposure to new markets and demographics where life and business are turning up the heat on creating the life of dreams with your eyes open.

27° Magazine will launch Spring of 2025 in conjunction with International Networking Events.

Why Join?

- Credibility - being published is one of the most important ways to gain SEO exposure
- Visibility in high-end outlets with prestigious printed magazines online
- Connection nationally and internationally
- Speaking opportunities
- Networking Collaboration and opportunities in our global mastermind
- Brand recognition
- Magazine will be published on Amazon globally for visibility featuring you as an author

What you will receive:
Your page will feature your professional photograph, your 500-word edited story, and contact information OR a 1-page advertisement that meets the specifications required.

Book a Consultation

We look forward to connecting with you to help you be seen, be heard and enter the new era of connection and collaboration.

Heather Andrews

Manufactured by Amazon.ca
Acheson, AB

14220347R00087